Japan Travel Guide:

Exploring the Land of Manga, Ramen, and Cherry Blossoms with Insights on Top Attractions, Local Eateries and Rich Cultural Experiences

By:
Leonora Thorne

© **Copyright 2024 - All rights reserved.**

The contents of this book may not be reproduced, duplicated, or transmitted without the direct written permission of the author or publisher.

Under no circumstances will the publisher or author be held liable for any damages, recovery, or financial loss due to the information contained in this book. Neither directly nor indirectly.

Legal Notice:

This book is protected by copyright. This book is for personal use only. You may not modify, distribute, sell, use, quote, or paraphrase any part or content of this book without the permission of the author or publisher.

Disclaimer Notice:

Please note that the information contained in this document is for educational and entertainment purposes only. Every effort has been made to present accurate, current, reliable, and complete information. No warranties of any kind are stated or implied. The reader acknowledges that the author is not offering legal, financial, medical, or professional advice. The contents of this book have been taken from various sources. Please consult a licensed professional before attempting any of the techniques described in this book.

By reading this document, the reader agrees that under no circumstances will the author be liable for any direct or indirect loss arising from the use of the information contained in this document, including but not limited to - errors, omissions, or inaccuracies.

Table of Contents

Introduction 4

Chapter 1: Travel Essentials 6

    Best time to visit. 8

    What to pack 10

    Getting there and moving around 12

    Practical information for visitors 13

Chapter 2: Must Visit Places in Japan 19

    1. Tokyo 19

    2. Osaka 22

    3. Kyoto 24

    4. Mount Fuji 26

    5. Hiroshima 27

    6. Nara 29

    7. Fukuoka 29

    8. Hakone 30

    9. Kanazawa 32

    10. Nikko 34

    11. Takayama 36

    12. Hakodate 38

    13. Nagoya 39

    14. Sapporo 42

15. Naoshima 44

16. Yokohama 44

17. Nagasaki 46

18. Kobe 48

Chapter 3: Itineraries 51

Chapter 4: Best Restaurants and Cuisine 56

Chapter 5: Accommodations in Japan 65

Chapter 6: Cultural Activities in Japan 70

Chapter 7: Nightlife And Festivals In Japan 74

Chapter 8: Souvenirs And Shopping in Japan 79

Must-Buy Souvenirs in Japan: 81

Chapter 9: Tips For Traveling in Japan 83

Conclusion 86

Introduction

Are you trying to find the greatest travel guide to assist you in making trip plans to Japan? Look no elsewhere! You will become acquainted with all of the treasures of this ancient nation by reading this comprehensive travel guide to Japan. Whether you're seeking for modern marvels or ancient customs, our guide is the ideal travel companion because he or she offers an in-depth and captivating tour of Japan.

Japan offers a plethora of breathtaking sites that will surprise you, since the past and modern cohabit together in this country. Imagine yourself standing in front of the stunning Mount Fuji, a revered and timeless symbol that has impacted artists, writers, and musicians for ages. Imagine yourself strolling through the bustling Nishiki Market in Kyoto, a global hub for foodies and travelers alike. Alternatively, you can enter the world of Studio Ghibli and learn about the magic involved in creating well-known animated films by going to the Ghibli Museum in Tokyo. These are only a handful of the countless amazing experiences Japan has in store for you.

What makes our trip guide superior to others? We understand that planning a trip can be difficult, but following our professional recommendations can help you avoid missing the best that Japan has to offer. Our comprehensive itineraries, smart maps, and wealth of information will ensure that you get the most out of every visit — first or fifty — whether it's your first.

Don't worry, while Japanese transportation can be confusing at times. Our book offers useful guidance on navigating the country's efficient rail system, including information on JR Passes for bullet trains and other useful modes of transit. To guarantee a hassle-free and seamless travel experience, we also provide information on recommended vaccinations and visa requirements.

In addition to the well-known tourist destinations, our itinerary includes visits to lesser-known locations and undiscovered gems. Drive through some of Japan's most breathtaking scenery, such as the captivating Japan Alps and the charming coastline roads of the Hokkaido Islands. To truly experience the culture, go to local celebrations and festivals, take a class in Japanese tea rituals, or even spend time in a temple. With the help of our guide, you will be able to truly connect with the spirit and heart of Japan.

Our guide is filled with information, but it's also updated frequently to provide you with the newest ideas and viewpoints. We put a lot of effort into making sure you have access to the most up-to-date information possible so you can make informed choices and create unforgettable experiences when traveling.

So why not wait? Make the most of Japan's magic by using our highly recommended travel guide. Let us be your trusted guide as you discover the rich fabric of Japanese customs, history, and contemporary wonders. Get ready for an adventure of a lifetime that will enthrall your senses and provide you with treasured memories.

Chapter 1: Travel Essentials

East Asia's Japan is an archipelago made up of many smaller islands as well as the four major islands of Honshu, Hokkaido, Kyushu, and Shikoku. Travelers from all over the world may easily reach it because of its advantageous location in the Pacific Ocean.

It's important to keep in mind that Japan is frequently thought of as an expensive travel destination while thinking about budgetary issues. However, cheap travel to Japan is feasible with careful preparation and research. When planning a vacation budget to Japan, there are a number of things to take into account:

1. Transportation: Buses, local trains, bullet trains, and other rail systems are all part of Japan's well-developed and effective transportation system. Consider getting a Japan Rail Pass for cheap travel on JR trains to save money on transportation, or choose less expensive choices like buses and regional flights.
2. Accommodations: Japan has a variety of lodging choices to fit a range of price points. When comparing prices, hostels,

Airbnb rentals, and traditional Japanese inns, or ryokans, can be more affordable options than five-star hotels. Affordably priced lodging can be found by making reservations in advance and doing internet price comparisons.

3. Meal: There are inexpensive dining options available in Japan, even if dining out in well-known tourist locations might be costly. Investigating neighborhood eateries such as conveyor belt sushi (kaitenzushi), shokudos (little informal restaurants), and izakayas (Japanese pubs) can offer genuine experiences at more affordable costs. Trying out inexpensive restaurants and paying attention to the locals' eating habits will help you control your food expenses.

4. Activities & Attractions: Japan offers visitors a diverse array of experiences thanks to its modern attractions, stunning natural settings, and rich cultural legacy. A lot of well-known tourist destinations, like parks, public gardens, and temples, provide inexpensive or free admission. You can control expenses by planning ahead of time and giving priority to attractions that suit your interests.

Japan is a sought-after tourist destination for several reasons. Here are a few factors that make it popular:

Japan is known for its distinctive blend of traditional customs and modern advancements, as well as its rich cultural legacy. In addition to taking in unique cultural practices like sumo wrestling and tea ceremonies, visitors may explore historic locations like temples and castles and immerse themselves in traditional arts.

Beautiful Scenes: Snow-capped mountains, picturesque countryside, vibrant cherry blossom gardens, and serene beaches are just a few of Japan's many breathtaking natural settings. Among the most popular attractions in the country are its iconic Mount Fuji, national parks, hot springs, and exquisite gardens.

Technological Advancements: Japan is renowned for its innovative urban design and architecture. When visiting major cities like Tokyo and Osaka, visitors may witness the newest innovations, including high-speed bullet trains, cutting-edge technology, and robots.

Japanese food is recognized for its variety, meticulous preparation, and high standards. In addition to sushi, Japanese cuisine also appeals to foodies, offering delicacies like tempura, sashimi, and ramen. Every visitor should try the cuisine and specialties of the region.

Overall, Japan appeals to travelers with a wide range of interests and financial constraints because of its unique blend of natural beauty, cutting-edge technology, rich cultural legacy, and gastronomic greatness. Travelers can manage their finances and have a good experience by carefully planning ahead of time and being open to exploring various parts of the nation.

When you are embarking on your Japanese vacation, there are a few things you should consider.

Best time to visit.

Depending on personal tastes, different seasons, tourist activities, crowds, and costs can influence the ideal time to visit Japan. To assist you in making a wise choice, I can provide you a few broad pointers.

Spring (March to May): Because of the pleasant weather and stunning cherry blossoms, spring is a popular season to visit Japan (sakura). Though it varies by location, Tokyo and Kyoto typically have their cherry blossom season in late March or early April. Additionally, spring is a fantastic season to visit gardens and outdoor attractions. But keep in mind that since this is the busiest travel season, there will be more people and more expensive lodging.

Fall: September through November is another season that is suggested for travel to Japan. There's gorgeous autumn foliage (koyo) in places like Kyoto, Nikko, and Hakone, and the temperature is moderate. When the fall colors are at their optimum in October, there are often less tourists in September and November. It's a great time to take part in outdoor activities, go to shrines and temples, and go to regional festivals.

Winter (December to February): Winter sports, hot springs (onsen), and snow festivals in prominent areas like Hokkaido and Nagano are just a few of the unique pleasures that Japan's winter has to offer. Additionally, there are typically less travelers throughout the winter, which might lead to better availability and more affordable lodging. But be careful to prepare appropriately; some areas can get rather chilly.

Summer (June to August): July and August can be particularly hot and muggy in Japan. On the other hand, if you appreciate summertime celebrations like the Gion Matsuri in Kyoto or the Nebuta Festival in Aomori, now is a perfect time to go. Additionally, you can travel to Hokkaido and Tohoku's northern regions, which have stunning natural settings and milder weather. Remember that summertime brings a lot of domestic travel, so popular destinations may get crowded.

The shoulder seasons of spring (March to May) and fall (September to November) typically offer a decent balance when taking crowds and affordability into account. The weather is usually nice during these periods, and you may take part in a variety of tourist activities without having to deal with the busiest times of the year — summer and cherry blossom season. It is suggested to book in early, nevertheless, as lodgings can still be in high demand.

What to pack

The time of year, the intended activities, and cultural customs should all be taken into account when packing for a trip to Japan. A thorough packing list for a vacation to Japan is provided below:

1. Clothing:
    - Seasonally appropriate clothing should be comfortable and breathable: summer clothing should be light and moisture-wicking, spring and fall clothing should be layerable, and winter clothing should be warm layers.
    - clothing that is modest and conservative, particularly while going to temples and other places of worship.
    - cozy walking shoes for tourism and city exploration.
    - If going to a hot spring or coastal area, wear swimwear.
2. Travel Documents:
    - a passport that is still valid for at least six months.
    - Copies of the itinerary, hotel bookings, and airline tickets, either in print or digital format.
    - Information on travel insurance.
    - If renting a car, you will need an international driver's license.
3. Electronics and Gadgets:
    - Power adapter or converter to charge electrical devices.
    - Smartphone, camera, or other gadgets for capturing memories.
    - For on-the-go charging, use a power bank or portable charger.
    - Earphones or headphones for entertainment during travel.

4. Medications and Health Essentials:
   - prescription drugs, if necessary, and the relevant paperwork.
   - Adhesive bandages, painkillers, motion sickness medications, and other supplies are included in a basic first aid pack.
   - any items required for personal hygiene.
5. Money
   - Sufficient local currency (Japanese Yen) or travel money card.
   - Credit/debit cards with international acceptance.
   - Wallet or money belt for keeping cash and cards secure.
6. Toiletries and Personal Care Items:
   - reusable liquid containers or travel-sized toiletries (shampoo, conditioner, body wash, toothpaste, etc.).
   - Use a washcloth or travel towel.
   - Wet wipes and hand sanitizer.
   - Depending on the season, lip balm, sunscreen, and bug repellent.
7. Miscellaneous:
   - For day outings, a lightweight daypack or backpack is ideal for transporting necessities.
   - maps or travel guides.
   - Rainfall is common throughout the year in Japan, so bring an umbrella or a small rain jacket.
   - Use a SIM card or portable Wi-Fi device to access the internet.
   - Travel locks to keep your bags safe.
   - To stay hydrated, use a reusable water bottle.
   - Snacks to have with you while touring or on the trip.

Getting there and moving around

The developed transportation system in Japan makes traveling to and within the country typically easy and efficient. Here are some details to aid your navigation:

- Public Transportation: Japan's public transportation system is renowned for its dependability, speed, and punctuality. It consists of a number of modes of transportation that provide extensive coverage inside and between cities and metropolitan areas, including trains, buses, taxis, and shinkansen (bullet trains).
- Trains: Trains are a frequent and useful mode of transportation in Japan. They are known for being punctual and routinely provide service, even in large cities. Although Japan Railways (JR) operates a large number of train lines, private railway companies operate in other regions. The Suica and PASMO are two examples of rechargeable smart cards, or IC cards, that make it easy to pay for buses and trains in a variety of locations.
- Bullet trains, or Shinkansen, are a type of high-speed rail system that links the main cities of Japan. It offers a rapid and efficient way to travel long distances, reaching high speeds of 320 km/h (199 mph). The Japan Rail Pass is a reasonably priced option for foreign visitors who want to take the shinkansen often.
- Buses: Buses complete the railroad network by providing service to areas that are challenging for trains to access. While short-distance buses go within cities and small towns, long-distance buses link different regions. The discounted Japan Bus Pass, which grants unlimited travel on pre-designated bus lines, is available to foreign visitors.
- Air Travel: Getting to remote areas or covering long distances rapidly can be accomplished by flying

domestically. Japan is home to several major airports, such as Haneda Airport in Tokyo, Kansai Airport in Osaka, and Narita Airport in Tokyo. If someone wants to travel within Japan, there are affordable domestic flight tickets available.

- Taxis are widely available and well-known for being dependable and clean in Japan. Taxis can be waved down on the street or found at taxi stands. Taxis are more commonly used for local travel or group excursions because they might be costly for long-distance transport.
- Rent a car: A foreign driver's license that is currently valid is required in order to rent a car in Japan. However, parking and traffic laws can be challenging, especially in urban areas. Car rentals are more common for travel to remote or rural locations with limited public transportation options.
- Bicycles: Bicycles are a prevalent mode of transportation in rural and smaller communities. Numerous cities provide bicycle rental services, allowing visitors to explore the area at their own leisure. But drive carefully, and only leave your bike in spots designated for that purpose.

Practical information for visitors

Language and communication

To get about Japan as a visitor, it's helpful to have a basic understanding of the language and modes of communication. Here are some details that will help you:

1. Language: Japanese is the official language of Japan. Even though many signage at prominent tourist locations have English translations and English is taught in schools, knowing a few basic Japanese phrases will still help you have a better experience and engage with locals.

2. Salutations: In Japanese society, salutations are highly valued. Depending on the time of day, it is usual to say "Ohayō gozaimasu" (Good morning) or "Konnichiwa" (Hello) when you first meet someone.
3. Basic Expressions: "Arigatō gozaimasu" (I'm grateful)
4. "Sumimasen": Pardon me or I'm sorry
5. "Kai wakarimasu eigo ga?" - Can you communicate in English?
6. "O-negai shimasu" means, kindly
7. "Iie": No; "Hai": Yes; "Gomen nasai": I apologize.
8. Honorific usage is significant since politeness is highly valued in Japanese culture. It is customary to address someone with "san" (e.g., Suzuki-san) after their name. Additionally, refrain from being very talkative or boisterous in public areas.
9. Public Transportation: Signs and announcements are typically posted in both Japanese and English when riding a rail or bus. To guarantee a comfortable travel, it is advisable to have a map with you or to know the names of your destinations in Japanese.
10. Tools for Translation: When you need help communicating, use translation tools on your smartphone, including Google Translate or specific apps for the Japanese language.
11. Cultural Etiquette: It's critical to comprehend and show respect for Japanese traditions and manners. Learn how to do things like take off your shoes before going inside, hold chopsticks properly, and bow when it's appropriate.
12. Emergency Phrases: It's important to know how to communicate in an emergency. Learn how to ask for help when you need it by knowing phrases like "Kyu-kei desu" (emergency) and "Tasukete!" (help!).

Currency and banking

- It is essential to understand money and banking in order to have a smooth financial trip to Japan. For visitors to Japan, the following information on money and banking is essential:
- Japan's official currency is the Japanese Yen (JPY). Because they usually offer favorable rates, it is advisable to exchange your money into JPY at one of the authorized foreign exchange counters, banks, or post offices.
- Acceptance of Cash: In Japan, cash is accepted practically everywhere, including restaurants, shops, and public transportation, and is used for the bulk of transactions. Having enough cash on hand is still crucial, even with the increasing usage of credit and debit cards, particularly when visiting isolated or smaller communities.
- ATMs: Japan has a reliable network of ATMs where you can get cash out using your international debit or credit card. ATMs are available at post offices, banks, and convenience stores. Find ATMs that take cards with international symbols on them, such as Mastercard, Visa, or Maestro. Because certain ATMs are only available for a limited period of time, make plans in advance.
- IC Cards: In Japan, rechargeable smart cards such as Suica or Pasmo are frequently utilized for minor purchases and transit. These cards can be helpful for quick purchases at convenience stores, vending machines, and public transportation. They can also be used to make small purchases at particular retailers.
- Exchange of Currencies: At major airports, banks, authorized exchange counters, or post offices, you can exchange your cash into Japanese Yen. It is wise to examine exchange rates and fees to make sure you are getting the best deal possible.

- Hours of Banking: In Japan, bank hours are typically 9:00 AM to 3:00 PM, Monday through Friday. Some banks may operate with fewer hours on Saturdays. It should be remembered that banks are closed on certain Japanese holidays, federal holidays, and weekends. Online banking services are helpful for managing your finances because they are available around-the-clock.
- Cards of Credit: Main credit cards including Visa, Mastercard, and American Express are frequently accepted in larger establishments, hotels, and eateries in urban areas. Even though carrying cash is generally a smart idea, it's conceivable that fewer small stores in remote areas accept credit cards.
- Apps for currency conversion: Consider downloading a currency conversion app to quickly compute prices and exchange rates on your smartphone. This can help with budgeting as well as knowing how much items are worth in your local currency.
- If you are an outsider visiting the nation, you can purchase goods without having to pay sales tax. You should look for stores that have signs saying "Tax-Free" or "Tourist Refund." To be eligible, you have to show your passport and complete a minimum purchase at participating establishments.

Safety

- It is imperative that visitors to Japan prioritize their safety at all times. Even while people generally perceive safety in Japan to be good, knowing the realities about safety is still essential to a successful and enjoyable vacation. To help you recall, keep the following in mind:
    - All-around Security: In Japan, where crime rates are generally low, violent crime is rare. But like with any

holiday, you should always exercise common sense and take safety precautions, such as keeping an eye on your belongings, especially when you're in crowded areas or using public transit.
- Natural disasters: In Japan, typhoons, earthquakes, and tsunamis happen often. Learn how to handle emergencies and follow the directions of the local authorities in the event of one. Be aware of the weather and pack accordingly if you're going somewhere that is prone to earthquakes or during typhoon season.
- The rules and legislation governing driving in Japan are extremely strict. Make sure you have a valid driver's license and an international driving permit if you plan to drive (IDP). Crossing streets should be done carefully because pedestrians in Japan drive on the left side of the road.
- Be cautious with your personal belongings, including your wallet, passport, and technological devices. Even though pickpocketing and theft are uncommon in Japan, it's wise to remain aware of your surroundings and protect your things.
- Health and Sanitation: Japan maintains stringent regulations about personal hygiene and sanitation. The tap water in the nation is safe to drink, although bottled water is readily available if you'd want. It's also advisable to have travel insurance that covers any medical emergency you may experience.
- Services for Emergencies: Call 119 to get through to the fire department or an ambulance in an emergency, and 110 to get through to the police. Even in situations where operators know English, it can be helpful to have key terms or locations written down in Japanese to facilitate effective communication.
- Culturally-based considerations: Be mindful of the national customs and traditions when visiting Japan. Learn the basic

rules of manners, like removing your shoes while entering certain establishments and bowing out of respect. Additionally, you should know how you conduct yourself in shrines and temples.

Chapter 2:
Must Visit Places in Japan

Japan is a fascinating nation that provides a singular fusion of historical customs and contemporary wonders. With its dynamic culture, breathtaking landscapes, rich history, and technical breakthroughs, Japan has grown in popularity as a travel destination for people all over the world.

To have an understanding of the variety of experiences Japan has to offer, it's beneficial to research the various cities and areas before making travel plans there. Here are a few noteworthy locations:

1. Tokyo

- Japan's vibrant metropolis, Tokyo, offers a plethora of activities, sights to see, and hidden treasures to unearth. Here is a thorough rundown of Tokyo that includes its main tourist destinations, happenings, and hidden treasures:
- Tokyo's top travel destinations include:

- Meiji Shrine: In a lush forest sits a serene Shinto shrine dedicated to Emperor Meiji and Empress Shoken. It provides a peaceful haven away from the bustling city.
- From its observation decks, the Tokyo Skytree — the tallest structure in Japan — offers breathtaking 360-degree views of the city.
- The most significant and ancient Buddhist temple in Tokyo is Senso-ji Temple. It features a magnificent main entrance, bustling market stalls, and traditional ceremonies.
- At the bustling Tsukiji Fish Market, patrons may savor freshly made sushi, see thrilling tuna auctions, and browse an array of culinary sellers.
- Renowned entertainment parks DisneySea and Tokyo Disneyland provide exhilarating rides, magical experiences, and beloved Disney characters.
- The Shinjuku Gyoen National Garden is a vast and beautifully landscaped area featuring cherry blossom trees, traditional Japanese gardens, and serene walking routes.
- Known as the "electric town," Akihabara is a hub for manga, anime, and electronic goods. It's a utopia for pop culture enthusiasts.
- Harajuku, a trendy district, is well-known for its unique street style, quirky shops, and Takeshita Street, which is packed with vibrant retailers.
- Shibuya Crossing: Known for its crowds of people and the interesting "scramble" of people attempting to cross the street in all directions, Shibuya Crossing is the intersection outside Shibuya Station.
- Tokyo Bay's artificial island, Odaiba, is home to cutting-edge retail establishments, entertainment venues, and breathtaking views of the waterfront.

Tourists Activities in Tokyo:

- Explore the bustling Tsukiji Outer Market, where you can find a wide variety of fresh seafood, street food, and traditional Japanese ingredients.
- Kindly visit teamLab Boundless: Immerse yourself in a world of interactive installations and digital art by visiting this state-of-the-art art gallery.
- Think about an elaborate tea ceremony: Take in the serene atmosphere and discover the art of preparing tea by visiting a traditional tea house.
- Explore the expansive Ueno Park, well-known for its zoo, museums, cherry blossoms, and Ueno Park fountain.
- Visit Tsukiji Fish Market for sushi: The freshest and best sushi in the area is served at the market's sushi restaurants.
- Explore Yanaka Ginza, a charming and historically significant shopping area brimming with local shops, food carts, and ancient buildings.
- To fully immerse oneself in the fantastical world of Studio Ghibli's cartoons, visit the Ghibli Museum. Special film screenings and interactive exhibits are available at this museum.
- To truly immerse yourself in the Japanese theatrical tradition known for its elaborate costumes and captivating storylines, take in a classic Kabuki performance.

Hidden Gems in Tokyo:

- Gotoku-ji Temple: A temple dedicated to statues of maneki neko, or beckoning cats, which are believed to bring good fortune and prosperity.
- The trendy neighborhood of Shimokitazawa is well-known for its unique boutiques, antique shops, and exciting nightlife.

- Kichijoji: Known for its famous Inokashira Park Zoo, charming cafes, gardens, and a bohemian atmosphere.
- Yanesen: Famous for its meandering lanes, medieval temples, and rural charm, Yanesen is comprised of the three historic districts of Yanaka, Nezu, and Sendagi.
- Tiny bars line the alleyways of Golden Gai, a small district in Shinjuku that offers a unique and private nightlife.
- Todoroki Valley in Tokyo is a beautiful and verdant retreat with a peaceful walking trail that winds alongside a small river and through dense foliage.
- Meguro River: A picturesque setting for a picnic or a leisurely stroll, the riverbanks are decked out with exquisite sakuratrees during cherry blossom season.

2. Osaka

- Osaka, a busy metropolis in Japan, is home to a variety of historical, modern, and cultural sites. Here are a few of Osaka's most popular landmarks, activities, and hidden gems:
- Osaka Castle, one of the most well-known castles in Japan and a must-see location, is well-known for its breathtaking architecture and attractive surroundings. Stroll around the castle's gardens and enjoy the observation deck's panoramic views.
- Osaka's most popular entertainment district, Dotonbori, is home to a diverse range of restaurants, food vendors, and retail stores. Taste local delicacies like takoyaki and okonomiyaki, and don't miss the iconic Glico Running Man sign.
- Universal Studios Japan is a well-known theme park with exhilarating rides, live shows, and attractions based on Universal Studios films and characters. Learn about the

Wizarding World of Harry Potter, Jurassic Park, and much more.

- Two well-known Osaka landmarks include the historic Shinsekai neighborhood and the well-known Tsutenkaku Tower. Explore conventional shops, savor street food, and take in the views from the observation deck atop the tower.
- Osaka Aquarium Kaiyukan, one of the largest aquariums in the world, is home to a variety of marine species, including penguins, dolphins, and whale sharks. Explore the many zones and the breathtaking Pacific Ocean tank.
- There are vendors selling fresh produce, fish, fruits, and street food at the bustling Kuromon Ichiba Market. Experience local delights and the vibrant atmosphere of this ancient market.
- Temple Shitennoji: One of the oldest temples in Japan, it was constructed in the sixth century. Explore the temple complex, enjoy the peaceful atmosphere, and admire the magnificent pagoda.
- Sumiyoshi Taisha is a stunning Shinto temple known for its unique architectural style and serene surroundings. Walk across the beautiful Sorihashi Bridge and explore the serene surroundings.
- Minoo Park is a stunning natural park located outside of Osaka. Explore hiking trails, waterfalls, and the vibrant foliage to make the most of the fall season. Because the famous Minoo Waterfall is so beautiful, it is a must-see.
- To experience living in Osaka during the Edo period, visit the Osaka Museum of Housing & Living. Explore the reconstructed streets, residences, and shops to learn about the city's history and culture.
- A charming alleyway lined with charming shops, cafes, and restaurants is Hozenji Yokocho. To find peace in the center of the city, head to Hozenji Temple, which is well-known for its moss-covered Mizukake Fudo figure.

- The Shin Umeda City Sky Building is an architectural marvel with a unique floating garden observatory that offers expansive views of Osaka. See the stunning cityscape when you arrive at dusk.
- Nakanoshima Park is a serene park located on an island between two rivers. Discover beautiful gardens, pathways, and old buildings like Osaka Central Public Hall and the Museum of Oriental Ceramics.
- The Kamigata Ukiyoe Museum is a hidden gem with traditional woodblock prints from the Edo period. Admire the magnificent artwork as you learn about the techniques and history of ukiyo-e printing.
- Discover the history, culture, and evolution of Osaka by visiting the interactive museum of history. Don't miss the magnificent view of Osaka from the museum's top floor.

3. Kyoto

- Kyoto, a city in Japan, is well known for its rich history, vibrant culture, and impressive architecture. Here are some of the tourist destinations, activities, and hidden treasures of Kyoto:
- Kiyomizu-dera Temple, a UNESCO World Heritage site, is well-known for its wooden terrace that offers expansive views of Kyoto and, in the spring, its breathtaking cherry blossoms.
- Tens of thousands of bright red torii gates line the roads that go through the forested Mount Inari, making Fushimi Inari Taisha a well-known Shinto shrine.
- Arashiyama Bamboo Forest is a serene bamboo grove that provides an excellent backdrop for peaceful walks and beautiful photographs.

- Kinkaku-ji (Golden Pavilion), a gorgeous Zen Buddhist temple draped in gold leaves, is surrounded by a calm garden and a motionless pond.
- Gion District: Renowned for its geisha district, this area of Kyoto is home to geisha and maiko (apprentice geisha), who can be seen meandering down the narrow alleyways lined with machiya homes.
- Beautiful grounds and "nightingale flooring," which chirp when people walk on them to alert others to intruders, are features of Nijo Castle, a UNESCO World Heritage Site.
- Enjoy a serene stroll along a canal flanked by thousands of cherry trees that burst into bloom in the springtime along the Philosopher's Path.
- The lively Nishiki Market is a traditional food market where over a hundred merchants and stalls sell foods and goods that are exclusive to Kyoto.
- Located in the heart of Kyoto's Gion district, the prominent Shinto shrine Yasaka Shrine is well-known for its vibrant festivals and lantern-lit evenings. The Zen temple Ginkaku-ji (Silver Pavilion) is well-known for its gorgeous grounds, unique sand garden, and the nearby serene "Path of Philosophy."

Hidden Gems in Kyoto:

- Tofuku-ji Temple: A serene temple well-known for its breathtaking autumnal scenery and quaint wooden bridge that spans a valley.
- A little-known temple with lovely grounds, a bamboo forest, tea houses, and an amazing light display at night is Kdai-ji Temple.
- Nestled in the bamboo grove of Arashiyama is the stunning Gio-ji Shrine, a moss temple with a calming atmosphere.

- Nijo Jinya is a historical samurai residence with beautifully preserved buildings, gardens, and displays showing Edo period samurai life.
- Nestled into the northern hills beyond Kyoto, the Kifune Shrine is a well-kept secret renowned for its peculiar water fortune-telling and picturesque environs.
- Otagi Nenbutsu-ji Temple is a lesser-known temple with over 1,200 quirky, expressive stone statues, all with their own distinct personalities.
- Renowned for its unique architectural features and tranquil surroundings, Kamigamo Shrine is among the most important and ancient Shinto shrines in Kyoto.

4. Mount Fuji

- Mount Fuji, a famous symbol of Japan, is a popular destination for hiking, sightseeing, and appreciating the area's natural beauty. Some of the sights and activities near Mount Fuji include the following:
- Climbing Mount Fuji: Take on the challenge of climbing Mount Fuji and enjoy breathtaking views from the summit during the climbing season's busiest months, July and August.
- Five Lakes in Fuji: Explore the Fuji Five Lakes area, which has hiking trails, hot springs, beautiful views of Mount Fuji, and outdoor activities like fishing and boating.
- See the picturesque Chureito Pagoda, which has a five-story pagoda and offers a well-known vista of Mount Fuji in the springtime surrounded by cherry blossoms.
- Fuji-Q Highland: Enjoy an exciting day at this theme park situated at the base of Mount Fuji, complete with exhilarating roller coasters and other attractions.

5. Hiroshima

- Hiroshima, a city in Japan, has a rich history and a diverse range of attractions. Here are some of the tourist destinations, things to do, and hidden treasures in Hiroshima:
- Peace Memorial Park is a noteworthy monument honoring the victims of the 1945 atomic strike. It houses the Atomic Bomb Dome and the Peace Memorial Museum in addition to several other monuments and memorials.
- The exquisite Japanese landscape Shukkeien Garden features tea houses, bridges, ponds, and meticulously manicured grounds. It offers a peaceful sanctuary in the heart of the city.
- Rebuilt, Hiroshima Castle features an observation deck with expansive views and a display of the city's history.
- An extensive examination of the atomic bombing, its aftermath, and the importance of promoting peace may be found at the Hiroshima Peace Memorial Museum.
- [3]
- Situated somewhat offshore from Hiroshima, Miyajima Island is well-known for being home to the Itsukushima Shrine and its iconic "floating" torii gate. Explore the island's breathtaking scenery, hiking trails, and friendly deer population.
- Mazda Museum: Explore the history and ingenuity of Mazda vehicles at this fascinating museum. See a selection of vintage vehicles and discover the creative ideas of the organization.
- The Hiroshima City Museum of Contemporary Art showcases contemporary art from Japan and other nations through a wide range of exhibitions and installations.
- Okonomimura: A multi-level building dedicated to the popular Hiroshima-style okonomiyaki dish. Explore a

variety of restaurants that provide various variations of this tasty pancake and enjoy the vibrant atmosphere.
- Scale the Hiroshima Orizuru Tower for a bird's-eye perspective over the surrounding mountains, Peace Memorial Park, and cityscape.
- Mitaki-dera Temple is a serene Buddhist temple set in the hills of Hiroshima. Discover the temple's gardens, walk along moss-covered walkways, and enjoy the calm atmosphere.
- If you love baseball, go see the zeal of the Hiroshima Carp supporters at a game at Mazda Zoom-Zoom Stadium Hiroshima.
- Enjoy breathtaking views of the surrounding islands and the city skyline by going on a boat tour or participating in water sports in Hiroshima Bay.

Hidden Gems:

- Hijiyama Park is a serene green space featuring cherry blossom trees, pathways, and an expansive view of Hiroshima city. It's a secret paradise for a leisurely stroll or picnic.
- The Mazda Museum of Ceramic Art is housed inside the Mazda corporate building and features a collection of modern ceramic artwork.
- The well-kept Hiroshima City Asa Zoological Park is home to a wide range of animals, such as elephants, giraffes, and lions. Spending a day there with family or animal lovers is highly recommended.
- Visit the bustling shopping districts of Kamiyacho and Hondori to discover the local cuisine, entertainment, and retail establishments.

- Momijidani Park: This park, which is situated on Miyajima Island, has beautiful fall foliage. Enjoy a leisurely stroll among the brilliant colors and calm surroundings.

6. Nara

- Numerous historical buildings and artworks can be found in Nara, which is sometimes regarded to as the cradle of Japanese civilization. A handful of Nara's attractions and things to do are as follows:
- Tōdai-ji Temple and Nara Park: Discover the pleasant deer in Nara Park and historical locations like Tdai-ji Temple, which is home to a massive bronze statue of the Great Buddha.
- See the Kofuku-ji Temple complex, which has structures and buildings that are over a millennium old, including the three-story pagoda and the Nan-endo octagonal hall.
- Nara National Museum: The museum houses a substantial collection of Buddhist artwork and antiquities, including pieces from the Nara period.
- Isuien Garden: Wander around this traditional Japanese garden, which has historic tea houses and beautiful seasonal scenery.
- Discover Horyu-ji Temple, one of the oldest wooden buildings in the world and a UNESCO World Heritage site. It has a substantial collection of Buddhist relics and artifacts.

7. Fukuoka

- Fukuoka is a vibrant city in Kyushu that is well-known for its delicious food, modern attractions, and fascinating history. Among the attractions and things to do in Fukuoka are:

- For a broad overview of the city and an appreciation of its historical significance, go visit the Fukuoka Castle Ruins.
- Explore Ohori Park, a large park featuring gardens, strolling paths, and boat rentals. It is constructed around a large pond.
- Enjoy the vast city views from the observation deck of Fukuoka Tower, which is particularly lovely at sunset.
- The large shopping and entertainment complex known as Canal City Hakata, which has theaters, shops, and restaurants, offers dining, entertainment, and shopping.
- You should take in the vibrant atmosphere of Yanagibashi Rengo Market, a thriving fish market where you may savor fresh seafood and local specialties.

8. Hakone

- A popular tourist destination in Japan, Hakone is known for its natural beauty, hot springs, and views of Mount Fuji. The following is a list of Hakone's tourist destinations, activities, and hidden gems:
- Situated on the banks of Lake Ashi, Hakone Temple is a picturesque Shinto shrine that is widely recognized for its iconic red torii gate that floats on the lake. Visitors are welcome to explore the temple grounds and enjoy the tranquil atmosphere and breathtaking views of the lake.
- Lake Ashi: This charming crater lake provides breathtaking views of Mount Fuji on clear days. Taking a boat cruise on the lake allows visitors to enjoy the beauty of the surrounding natural environment.
- Open-Air Museum in Hakone: Displaying a range of contemporary sculptures and artwork, this outdoor exhibition is situated within the stunning foliage of Hakone. This place offers visitors a unique and imaginative experience.

- Owakudani, a volcanic valley noted for its hot springs and active sulfur vents, is frequently referred to as the "Great Boiling Valley." Visitors can take a ropeway to Owakudani and observe the steam rising from the earth. It's a great place to enjoy broad vistas of the surrounding volcanic landscape.
- Hakone Ropeway: Offering passengers panoramic views of Mount Fuji, Lake Ashi, and the Hakone region, the Hakone Ropeway offers a scenic excursion over the crater-filled Owakudani valley. To fully appreciate the area's grandeur, this is a must-do activity.
- Hakone Checkpoint provides a glimpse into Japan's feudal past as a historic checkpoint on the famed Tokaido road. In addition to learning about the history of the area and taking pictures in traditional samurai attire, visitors can explore the restored checkpoint buildings.
- The stunning grounds of the Hakone Venetian Glass Museum house an impressive collection of artwork made of Venetian glass. Visitors can view intricate glass sculptures, the history of glassmaking, and even watch demonstrations of glassblowing.
- Hakone Pirate Ship: Sailing the Hakone Pirate Ship is an exciting and distinctive way to discover Lake Ashi. With their pirate galleon-style construction, the ships provide picturesque vistas of the surrounding mountains and lake.
- Hakone Onsen: The area is home to a large number of ryokans, or traditional Japanese inns, and onsen (hot spring) resorts. Hakone is well-known for its hot springs. Immersion in Japanese culture and relaxation in a traditional hot spring bath are ideal.
- The Hakone Museum of Art is renowned for its collection of Asian art and Japanese ceramics. Beautiful ceramics, pleasant garden exploration, and a calm atmosphere await visitors.

Hidden Gems:

- Hakone Detached Palace Garden is a secret treasure nestled in the forest. It features lovely seasonal flowers and traditional Japanese architecture in a tranquil and serene setting.
- The Hakone Sekisho Exhibition Hall is a tiny museum that chronicles the checkpoint's history and its significance during the Edo period. It sheds light on the history of the area and the significance of the checkpoint system.
- Hakone Botanical Garden of Wetlands: a botanical garden with an emphasis on wetland plants that provides a serene setting with a variety of walking trails and lovely vegetation.
- Amazake-chaya Tea House: This is a traditional tea house where guests can unwind in a tranquil woodland while sipping amazake, a sweet fermented rice beverage.
- Hakone Kowakien Yunessun: An unusual theme park with hot springs that offers a variety of baths, including ones infused with coffee, wine, and green tea. For fans of hot springs, it's an interesting and enjoyable experience.

9. Kanazawa

- Located on Japan's largest island, Honshu, in the Ishikawa Prefecture, is this breathtaking city. With its well-preserved Edo-period neighborhoods, traditional gardens, and historical sites, Kanazawa blends natural beauty with cultural legacy. The following is a list of things to do in Kanazawa, events to attend, and hidden gems to discover:
- Kenroku-en Garden: Kenroku-en is a beautifully landscaped garden featuring ponds, teahouses, and strolling paths. It is considered to be one of Japan's top three

gardens. The seasons of cherry blossoms and fall foliage are particularly lovely.
- Discover the grounds of the beautifully renovated Kanazawa Castle, which is home to several historic buildings and gorgeous gardens. The castle illuminates the area's feudal past while providing expansive views of the metropolis.
- Discover the charming alleyways of the Higashi Chaya neighborhood, a geisha district renowned for its old wooden teahouses. Take advantage of the opportunity to learn about geisha culture, traditional performances, and tea ceremonies.
- Omicho Market: Enjoy the vibrant atmosphere of this busy seafood market, which sells a variety of fresh fish as well as local products and specialties. Speak with local vendors and try out some local delights.
- Visit the 21st Century Museum to learn about modern art. It is well-known for its innovative displays and unusual circular construction. In addition to exhibitions by Japanese and international artists, the museum has interactive installations.
- The Nagamachi neighborhood was once home to samurai residences, providing a window into the past for tourists. Gain insight into the samurai way of life by exploring the historic homes, meandering streets, and Nomura Samurai House.
- Learn about the mysteries of Myoryuji Temple, sometimes referred to as the Ninja Temple. This cleverly constructed building offers an intriguing insight at ninja design with its hidden chambers, trap doors, and secret pathways.
- To find out more about the teachings and legacy of well-known Zen philosopher Daisetz Suzuki, visit the D.T. Suzuki Museum. The museum has a serene atmosphere with exhibits related to Zen Buddhism.

- Wander through the less-traveled-by geisha district of Nishi Chaya, which is home to restored shops, galleries, and teahouses. Savor wagashi and matcha tea while admiring the traditional atmosphere (Japanese sweets).
- Discover more about the age-old craft of creating gold leaf in Kanazawa by visiting the Yasue Gold Leaf Museum. Discover the techniques, background, and intricate gold leaf artwork.
- To witness the beauty of Kutaniyaki ceramics, go to the Kutaniyaki Art Museum. Savor the vibrant colors and ornate accents of this local custom.
- See Oyama Shrine, which is well-known for its massive torii gate and amazing city vistas. Take your time exploring the shrine's grounds and soaking in the calm atmosphere.
- Discover the world of Noh drama with an invitation from the Kanazawa Noh Museum. Learn about the history, costumes, masks, and musical accompaniment of this traditional Japanese theater.
- Ishikawa Prefectural Museum of Art: Learn more about the prefecture's artistic and cultural traditions by visiting the Ishikawa Prefectural Museum of Art. A vast array of both international and Japanese artwork is on show at the museum.
- Steer off the main road to see Utasu Shrine, a hidden gem nestled in a peaceful residential area. Saunter into the little forest that surrounds the shrine and take in the serenity and quiet.

10. Nikko

- In Japan's Tochigi Prefecture, the quaint town of Nikko is well-known for its serene surroundings, fascinating historical sites, and stunning natural beauty. The list of tourist destinations, activities, and hidden treasures in Nikko that follows includes:

- Toshogu Temple: Toshogu Shrine, a UNESCO World Heritage site, is one of Japan's most ornate shrines with intricate sculptures and vibrant colors. It is the last resting place of the founder of the shogunate, Tokugawa Ieyasu.
- Large natural park with hiking trails, mountains, lakes, and waterfalls is called Nikko National Park. The scenery is stunning, particularly in the fall when the leaves are turning color.
- Nestled among Nikko's peaks lies a serene body of water called Lake Chuzenji. Visitors can enjoy boat excursions, strolls around the lake, and amazing views of the surrounds.
- Kegon Falls, one of the most well-known waterfalls in Japan, plunges about 97 meters into a slender canyon. The fall season is particularly lovely.
- One of Nikko's hidden gems is Kanmangafuchi Abyss, which is well-known for its lovely walking trail along the riverbed and various "Jizo" stone statues surrounding it. During cherry blossom season, the location is particularly scenic.
- The iconic crimson Shinkyo Bridge spans the Daiya River and acts as the entrance to Nikko's temples and shrines. It is a popular spot for photographs and is revered as a holy bridge.
- Exquisite antiques and statues may be found at the historical Buddhist temple Rinnoji Temple. It is the most important temple in Nikko and is associated with the Toshogu Shrine.
- The Taiyuinbyo Mausoleum honors Tokugawa Iemitsu, the third ruler of the Tokugawa shogunate. The Five-Story Pagoda and Yomeimon Gate are two examples of its exquisite architecture.

- Many different kinds of plants and flowers, including rare species, can be found at the serene Nikko Botanical Garden. Outdoor enthusiasts and photographers will love it there.
- The Nikko Woodcarving Center is a place to experience the traditional woodcarving method, complete with classes and exhibits featuring intricate wooden creations created by local artists.
- Yumoto Onsen is a hot spring resort featuring peaceful hot spring pools, gorgeous natural settings, and traditional ryokan accommodations. It is located in the mountains of Nikko.
- The Irohazaka Winding Road leads to the scenic Ryuzu Waterfall. The seasons of spring and fall are especially fascinating.
- Chuzenji Temple is a small temple near Lake Chuzenji that is well-known for its calm atmosphere and amazing views of the surrounding mountains and lake.
- The Akechidaira Ropeway is a cable car that takes passengers to a panoramic observation platform with breathtaking views of Lake Chuzenji and the surrounding mountains.

11. Takayama

- Takayama is a charming old town in the Japanese Alps that is well-known for its old town, customs, and local handicrafts. The following are some of Takayama's tourism destinations, activities, and hidden treasures:
- Sanmachi Suji: Explore the quaint streets of Sanmachi Suji, Takayama's historic district. This neighborhood, which is bordered with tastefully kept traditional wooden houses, sake breweries, local shops, and cafes, may give you an idea of the town's rich history and culture.

- See Takayama Jinya, a former government building that functioned as the administrative center of the area during the Edo period. It presently functions as a museum, providing details about the manner of life and town government of that era.
- Take in the vibrant atmosphere of the Takayama Morning Market, where regional sellers provide a range of products, such as fresh fruit, crafts, and cuisine. It's a great place to shop for souvenirs and try the local cuisine.
- Explore the outdoor museum Hida Folk Village (Hida no Sato), which features traditional thatched-roof houses from the Hida area. Investigate the village to learn more about the rural way of life and handicrafts of the area.
- If you visit Takayama in the spring or fall, make sure not to miss the Takayama Festival—one of the most famous and magnificent festivals in Japan. It has lovely floats, traditional music and dance performances, and an enjoyable atmosphere.
- Discover the magnificent wooden Takayama Old Town Hall, which once held the town's administrative buildings. Today, it houses a museum with artifacts from the past that illustrate the development of the town.
- Trek to Shiroyama Park, which has a hilltop view of Takayama. From a distance, the town and its environs offer some of the most beautiful views, particularly during the cherry blossom season in the spring and the fall foliage change.
- Wander around the bustling Miyagawa Morning Market, where local vendors sell a range of products like baked pastries, fresh fruit, and crafts. It's a great place to try local street food and mingle with the friendly locals.
- To find out more about the traditional celebration floats used during the Takayama Festival, visit the Takayama

Yatai Kaikan. Discover the significance of the meticulous craftsmanship and history of these remarkable floats.
- Higashiyama Walking Course: Take a stroll along the lovely Higashiyama Walking Course, which winds past serene woodlands, temples, and shrines. Enjoy the peaceful atmosphere and immerse yourself in nature as you explore Takayama's lesser-known attractions.

12. Hakodate

- Hakodate is the southernmost city on the Japanese island of Hokkaido. It combines the charm of history, beautiful scenery, and delicious seafood. Here are some of the tourist destinations, activities, and hidden treasures of Hakodate:
- Bay of Hakodate: The city's surrounding area is well known for its charming harbor, which offers breathtaking views of Mount Hakodate, the surrounding mountains, and the city skyline. Admire the magnificent view as you stroll around the waterfront.
- Mount Hakodate is a popular site that offers expansive views of the bay and city. Hiking trails and ropeways are the two ways that visitors can reach the peak. The view from the observation deck is especially stunning at night.
- In addition to being a historical monument, the star-shaped fort known as Goryokaku is a symbol of Hakodate. It was built in the 1800s and is well known for its magnificent springtime cherry blossoms. Take in the aerial view of the fort's grounds from the top of the Goryokaku Tower, and discover its past at the nearby Goryokaku History Museum.
- The Motomachi District is renowned for its churches, historic buildings, and international consulates. The district is charming and features a fusion of Western and Japanese design elements. Wander through the narrow streets, visit

the Old Public Hall in the Hakodate Ward, and enjoy the unique atmosphere.
- The Hakodate Morning Market is a lively place to acquire a wide variety of fresh seafood, including the well-known Hakodate squid. Sample regional cuisines, savor seafood bowls for breakfast, and strike up a conversation with friendly vendors.
- The Hakodate City Museum of Northern Peoples offers information on the history and traditional ways of life of the Ainu people of Hokkaido. Examine exhibits of traditional clothing, art, and artifacts.
- Nestled in the quiet hills of Hakodate sits the Trappistine Monastery, where a community of Catholic nuns resides. Customers purchase the nuns' handmade goods and confections, as they are well-known for their confectionery expertise.
- At Yunokawa Onsen, one of Hakodate's hot spring resorts, relax and rejuvenate. In Yunokawa Onsen, you can take advantage of the therapeutic effects of natural hot springs in any of the public baths or traditional Japanese ryokans.
- Kanemori's Red Brick Warehouse: Shops, restaurants, and galleries may be found at the beachfront Kanemori Red Brick Warehouse, which has a nostalgic feel. Savor the lively atmosphere, shopping for local products, and dining at waterfront restaurants.
- Take a trip to Hakodate's tropical botanical garden to escape to a tropical paradise. Take in the serene ambiance while discovering a variety of plant species, including uncommon flowers and trees.

13. Nagoya

- The vibrant city of Nagoya is located in central Japan. As the capital of Aichi Prefecture, it is the country's fourth-largest city. This is a synopsis of Nagoya that covers its events, tourism sites, and hidden treasures:

- Restored to its former splendor, Nagoya Castle boasts breathtaking architecture and an intriguing past. It's among the most popular attractions in Nagoya. Visitors are welcome to explore the castle's grounds, learn about its samurai past, and enjoy the expansive views from the summit.
- The Atsuta Shrine One of the most important Shinto shrines in all of Japan, this treasured historical site houses the sacred sword "Kusanagi-no-Tsurugi." It has beautiful gardens that are perfect for a leisurely stroll and a serene atmosphere.
- Situated near to the Osu Kannon Temple, the bustling Osu Shopping District is home to a variety of shops, restaurants, and arcades. It's a pleasant place to enjoy some regional cuisine and peruse unique items and antiques.
- Railway enthusiasts will love this museum, which is dedicated to trains, Railway Park, and SCMAGLEV. With its enormous collection of both modern and vintage trains, interactive exhibits, and simulators, it provides an intriguing view into Japan's railway past.
- Popular with families, the Nagoya City Science Museum offers interesting exhibits and displays on a variety of scientific topics, including robots, space exploration, and natural history. The star attraction is the world's largest planetarium, which offers amazing astronomical displays.
- Located near Nagoya Castle, the Tokugawa Art Museum showcases artwork and artifacts from one of the most well-known samurai families in Japan. Strolling around the beautiful gardens, visitors can admire the assortment of historical relics.

- Nagoya TV Tower: With a height of 180 meters, this observation tower offers expansive views of the city. The lit Nagoya skyline is particularly stunning at night.
- Nagoya Port: There are other attractions in the port neighborhood, including as the previously mentioned Railway Park and SCMAGLEV, in addition to the Nagoya Port Aquarium, which is home to a diverse array of marine life. It's also a great place for seaside dining establishments and promenade walks.
- The Nagoya City Art Museum's collection of modern and contemporary art, which features works by well-known Japanese and international artists, will appeal to art enthusiasts. Furthermore, the museum holds events with an artistic focus.
- Planetarium at Nagoya City Science Museum: Located within the same building as the museum, this planetarium provides immersive shows that take visitors on fascinating cosmic journeys. It's the perfect place to learn about astronomy and witness breathtaking space exploration.

Hidden Gems in Nagoya:

- Osu Kannon Temple: Nestled in the busy Osu neighborhood, this temple offers a tranquil haven from the bustle of the city. It has a serene garden with a lovely pagoda.
- Shirotori Garden: Located in Tokugawaen Park in Nagoya, this undiscovered gem offers a typical Japanese landscape complete with bridges, ponds, and teahouses. It's a calm place to take in the scenery and discover Japanese design.
- Noritake Garden: A lovely park featuring gardens, a museum, and shops has been created on the site of a former factory. In addition to learning about Noritake's history, visitors can even try painting their own ceramics.

- The unique Nagoya City Tram & Subway Museum honors the city's tram and subway networks while providing a window into its transit past. In addition to learning about the history of the subway, visitors can experience operating a vintage tram.
- Nagoya City Archives: The archives offer a wealth of historical records, images, and maps pertaining to the past of the city, making them a valuable resource for history buffs. It's an interesting tool for learning about Nagoya's past.

14. Sapporo

- Renowned for its unique attractions, delicious food, and stunning natural beauty, Sapporo is a bustling Japanese city. Here are a few of Sapporo's most popular tourist destinations, happenings, and hidden treasures:
- Odori Park, the city's main park, is the site of several annual events, including the well-known Sapporo Snow Festival in the winter.
- To get a broad perspective of the city and the surrounding mountains, ascend to the Sapporo TV Tower observation deck.
- Visit the Sapporo Beer Museum to discover the brewing history and method of one of Japan's oldest and most recognizable beer brands, Sapporo beer.
- Mount Moiwa Ropeway: Take a delightful cable car ride up Mt. Moiwa for breathtaking views of Sapporo, especially after nightfall.
- Discover more about the world of Hokkaido's well-known Shiroi Koibito cookies by taking advantage of the factory tours, museum visits, and lovely European-style gardens available at Shiroi Koibito Park.

- Hokkaido Shrine: This calm Shinto shrine is situated in the center of the city and is particularly beautiful in the spring when the cherry blossoms are in bloom.
- See the historic Sapporo Clock Tower, which serves as both the city's symbol and a little historical museum.
- Explore Susukino, the part of Sapporo known for its vibrant nightlife, clubs, dining options, and retail establishments.
- To get away from the heat or cold, explore the vast underground shopping and dining complex situated beneath the city of Sapporo.
- Explore the Hokkaido University Botanic Garden, a quaint park with a wide variety of plants and flowers, including a gorgeous avenue of cherry blossoms.
- Nakajima Park is a large park near Sapporo's city center. Enjoy a stroll around the lake or rent a paddleboat to go around it.
- Hokkaido's Historical Village: This outdoor museum allows visitors to travel back in time and experience traditional Hokkaido life through the reconstruction of buildings from the late 19th and early 20th centuries.
- Moerenuma Park is a large park designed by renowned artist Isamu Noguchi that combines art, nature, and play areas to provide a unique and immersive experience.
- Sapporo Winter Sports Museum: Learn about the history of Sapporo's involvement in winter sports and the Winter Olympics through interesting exhibits and displays.
- See the famed Hokkaido Shrine located on the grounds of Maruyama Park, which is known for its massive, historic cherry trees.

15. Naoshima

- Naoshima, an inland sea island in Seto, is well known for its modern art museums, buildings, and sculptures. Among the sights and things to do on Naoshima Island are:
- Discover the remarkable modern art museum called Chichu Art Museum, created by architect Ando Tadao and housing pieces by Claude Monet, Walter De Maria, and James Turrell.
- Take part in the Art House Project and explore the various art installations dotted throughout a small port town on Naoshima Island.
- Views of the Seto Inland Sea can be enjoyed while visiting the Benesse House, a hotel and art gallery that features modern art.
- Lee Ufan Museum: Visit this specialized museum on Naoshima Island to view the artwork of Korean artist Lee Ufan.
- I Love Yu: Take pleasure in a singular experience at I Love Yu, a public bathhouse that also functions as a piece of art made by Shinro Ohtake.

16. Yokohama

Yokohama, Japan, a bustling metropolis with a variety of tourist sites, festivals, and hidden gems, is located just south of Tokyo. This is a thorough introduction to Yokohama:

Tourism Highlights:

- Yokohama's modernism is embodied in the waterfront district of Minato Mirai 21, which is home to iconic buildings including the Landmark Tower, Cosmo Clock 21, and Red Brick Warehouse. It offers dining options,

- entertainment, retail therapy, and stunning views of the city skyline.
- Yamashita Park is a quaint park by the water with lush vegetation, meandering walks, and picturesque port views. In the park is also the well-known Hikawa Maru, a former ocean liner that is currently used as a museum.
- Yokohama, one of the largest Chinatowns in the world, features lively streets, traditional Chinese architecture, and a wide selection of restaurants, shops, and food carts.
- A traditional Japanese garden, Sankeien Garden features stunning views, historic buildings, and in-season flowers. It provides a tranquil escape from the city and is particularly lovely during the cherry blossom season.
- Situated on a stunning island is Yokohama Hakkeijima Sea Paradise, a theme park and aquarium complex. It offers a range of attractions, such as thrilling rides, fun shows, and the opportunity to get up close and personal with aquatic life.

Activities:

- The Cup Noodles Museum is a one-of-a-kind institution dedicated to the history and evolution of instant ramen. In addition to learning how noodles are manufactured, visitors can make their own cup noodles and explore interactive installations.
- Enjoy expansive views across Yokohama and beyond from the observation deck of the Yokohama Landmark Tower Sky Garden. It is located in the Landmark Tower on the 69th level. On a clear day, you might even be able to see Mount Fuji in the distance.
- Once a customs building, the Yokohama Red Brick Warehouse is now home to shops, galleries, and event

spaces. It's a great place to shop for souvenirs and enjoy live entertainment.
- Yokohama Stadium hosts concerts and other events in addition to being the home field for the baseball team. Sports lovers in this area watch baseball games on a regular basis.

Hidden Gems:

- Yokohama Omoshiroi Pier: This little pier, which is close to Osanbashi Pier, is a tranquil place to take in the bay views, see cruise ships passing by, and unwind away from the bustle.
- Iseyama Kotai Shrine: Nestled in a residential neighborhood, this undiscovered shrine is renowned for its lovely landscape and serene ambience. It's a calm location where you may get away from the busy metropolis and experience Japanese spirituality.
- Soji-ji Temple: A calm Buddhist temple with striking wooden constructions and a tranquil landscape. Away from the tourist throng, it's a hidden treasure that provides an opportunity for peaceful thought and introspection.
- Kanazawa Bunko: An antique book and cultural artifact collection housed in a historic library and museum. It's a little-known destination where you may get a tranquil, quiet look into the literary heritage of Japan.

17. Nagasaki

- Southwest The city of Nagasaki in Japan has a rich cultural legacy, a lengthy history, and breathtaking scenery. Here are some of the tourist destinations, activities, and hidden treasures of Nagasaki:

- Visit the Nagasaki Peace Park, which is devoted to fostering peace and honoring the people who perished when the atomic bomb was dropped on the city in 1945. It also houses the Atomic Bomb Museum. The Atomic Bomb Museum offers a moving and instructive look at the effects of the bomb.
- Discover Glover Garden, a neighborhood of Western-style homes with a view of Nagasaki Harbor. This outdoor museum displays how foreign people and traders influenced the city's architecture and culture.
- Nagasaki Chinatown: Explore Shinchi Chinatown, the energetic Chinatown in Nagasaki, to take in the colorful architecture, mouthwatering cuisine, and bustling environment.
- Mount Inasa: For a sweeping perspective of Nagasaki, drive or ride a cable car to the summit of Mount Inasa. Particularly around dusk, the observation deck provides amazing views over the city.
- Visit the Nagasaki Peace Memorial Hall for the Atomic Bomb Victims, a space dedicated to introspection and contemplation of the bomb's effects. It includes first-person accounts, images, and bombing-related exhibits.
- Discover the historical island of Dejima, which functioned as a trading post for Japan during its period of isolation. It provides information about the nation's interactions with other cultures as well as Nagasaki's growth as a global port city.
- Visit Oura Church, a stunning Catholic church that was influential in the development of Christianity in Japan. It was one of the few locations where Christians continued to practice their faith although it was outlawed across the nation.
- One of Japan's biggest lantern celebrations, the Nagasaki Lantern Festival, is something you shouldn't miss if you're

in the area in February. Savor the street food vendors, traditional performances, and beautiful lantern displays.
- Kujukushima Islands: Explore the stunning Kujukushima Islands by kayak or cruise. This group of 208 small islands is well-known for its diverse marine life and gorgeous scenery. It's a fantastic chance for outdoor enthusiasts and lovers of the natural world.
- Explore the rich cultural legacy and history of Nagasaki at the Museum of History and Culture. Interactive exhibitions, artwork, and artifacts depict the city's varied past.

18. Kobe

- Kobe, a vibrant city in Japan, offers a wealth of activities, stunning landscape, and an intriguing past. The following are some of the best sights, activities, and hidden places in Kobe:
- Kobe Port Tower: An iconic landmark and municipal emblem, it offers an observation deck with panoramic views of Kobe and the surrounding area.
- Kitano-cho: This neighborhood is well-known for its "ijinkan," or European-style homes, which were formerly the homes of foreign traders and diplomats. Many of these homes are now museums, cafes, and retail establishments.
- Kobe Harborland is a waterfront neighborhood including eateries, retail centers, and performance spaces. It's a wonderful area to promenade, take in the scenery, and eat at one of the waterfront eateries.
- Situated on the foothills of Mount Rokko, the Kobe Nunobiki Herb Gardens boast an array of vibrant flowers and herbs. To get to the gardens and take in the stunning surroundings, take a cable car trip.

- Mount Rokko: Known for its amazing views of Kobe and the surroundings, Mount Rokko is a well-liked spot for trekking and outdoor enjoyment.
- Kobe Chinatown, also called Nankin-machi, is a bustling neighborhood full with Chinese eateries, retail establishments, and tourist destinations. It's a fantastic spot to sample some scrumptious Chinese food.
- Kobe Beef: Kobe is well-known for its premium beef, or "Kobe beef." Don't forget to sample this treat at one of the city's well-known steakhouses.
- Arima Onsen: One of Japan's most well-known and historic hot spring towns, Arima Onsen is close to Kobe. Bathe in the natural hot springs and revitalize yourself while taking in the breathtaking mountain views.
- The longest suspension bridge in the world, the Akashi Kaikyo Bridge links Awaji Island with Kobe. Maiko Marine Promenade, an observation platform inside the bridge, offers panoramic views of the structure.
- Sorakuen Garden: An exquisite Japanese garden featuring tea houses, ponds, and lovely scenery. It is a tranquil haven within the bustling metropolis.
- Kobe Earthquake Memorial Museum: This museum honors the Great Hanshin-Awaji Earthquake of 1995 and offers information on the catastrophe and Kobe's effects.
- Shin-Kobe Ropeway: Enjoy a breathtaking ride up Mount Maya on the ropeway, where you can take in expansive views of Kobe and the surroundings.
- Kobe City Museum: Through a variety of exhibitions and exhibits, discover Kobe's history and culture.
- Nunobiki Falls: A quartet of cascades situated near Mount Rokko. You can hike to the falls and take in the splendor of nature.

- The Kobe Oji Zoo is home to a diverse range of species, such as lions, elephants, and pandas. It's a fantastic location for family outings with children.
- Sake breweries in Kobe's Nada District: The Nada District is well-known for producing sake. Learn about the process of manufacturing sake and try various types by taking a tour of one of the breweries.
- See a variety of marine life, such as sea turtles, dolphins, and penguins, at the Kobe City Suma Marine Aquarium.
- One of the oldest Shinto temples in Japan, Ikuta Shrine is renowned for its exquisite construction and tranquil setting.
- The Kobe Anpanman Children's Museum & Mall is an entertaining and interactive children's museum that showcases the well-known Japanese figure Anpanman.
- Kobe Luminarie: This yearly light festival, which takes place in December, is a must-see for anybody visiting Kobe. It features stunning light displays that illuminate the city.

Chapter 3: Itineraries

An itinerary is essential when planning a trip to Japan for several reasons:

Effective use of time: From vibrant cities like Tokyo and Osaka to tranquil settings like Kyoto and Mount Fuji, Japan offers a wide range of sights and experiences to discover. By planning out the locations you want to see, an itinerary helps you make the most of your time and guarantees you don't miss any must-see attractions or activities.

Cost control: Japan is a costly travel destination despite having a good standard of living. You can study and compare prices for lodging, activities, and transportation by planning your itinerary in advance. This enables you to make wise financial decisions and identify opportunities for savings, such purchasing inexpensive lodging or taking use of transportation passes at a discount.

Setting priorities and personalizing your itinerary: With so many sights and activities to choose from, planning a trip to Japan may be rather difficult. An itinerary assists you in setting priorities for the locations and pursuits that suit your interests, be they visiting historical sites, savoring delectable cuisine, or taking in breathtaking scenery. To maximize your vacation experience, you can customize your itinerary to fit your tastes.

Easy navigation: Trains, buses, and subways are all part of Japan's well-connected transportation network. You may plan your travels, comprehend the logistics of getting from one point to another, and maximize your trip time by using an itinerary. It might also assist you in deciding if your itinerary would benefit from obtaining a Japan Rail Pass, which offers unlimited travel on JR trains.

Cultural immersion: You can incorporate immersive experiences that represent the customs and traditions of Japan by designing an itinerary that includes trips to temples, tea ceremonies, traditional markets, and cultural festivals. Japan is a country with a rich cultural legacy. By adding these components to your itinerary, you'll be able to comprehend and value Japan's distinct culture even more.

Peace of mind and adaptability: A schedule is necessary, but it's also critical to allow for adaptability and spontaneity. You might need to modify your plans as a result of unforeseen circumstances or discoveries made along the route. But knowing that you have a basic plan to follow gives you a sense of organization and peace of mind when you start with a well-designed schedule.

When making an itinerary for your trip to Japan, don't forget to take your hobbies, preferred pace, and style of travel into account. By doing this, you can get the most out of your trip, stretch your money and time, and produce priceless memories in this intriguing nation.

Here is a suggested **one-week itinerary** for your trip to Japan:

Day 1: Tokyo

- Tokyo, the capital and largest city of Japan, is a great place to start your journey.
- Experience the vibrant atmosphere of the world's largest fish market, Toyosu Fish Market.
- Discover the Sensoji Temple, a stunning Buddhist temple located in Asakusa that is well-known for the Kaminari Gate.

- Savor the vibrant nightlife of Golden Gai, a maze of backstreet bars.
- Possible day trip: Take a look at Kamakura to see the enormous Buddha statue (Daibutsu) and tour the ancient temples.

Day 2: Tokyo

- Take an additional day to explore Tokyo's diverse culture and iconic sites.
- Take a leisurely stroll around the grounds of the Imperial Palace.
- If there is a sumo match during your visit, go to see it (tickets sell out quickly).
- Discover neighborhoods that are well-known for their distinctive atmosphere, food options, and shopping, such as Shinjuku, Shibuya, or Harajuku.
- Savor delectable Japanese cuisine at neighborhood eateries or check out stand-alone sushi bars like Uogashi Nihon-Ichi.

Day 3-4: Kyoto

- Visit Kyoto, a city well-known for its ancient charm and extensive history.
- Discover Kyoto's gardens and temples, which include the well-known Fushimi Inari Taisha and Kinkaku-ji (Golden Pavilion).
- Learn about Japanese cooking by enrolling in a class and making some of the country's signature dishes.
- Stroll through the Bamboo Grove of Arashiyama and pay a visit to the renowned Tenryu-ji Temple.
- In the Gion neighborhood of Kyoto, take in the splendor of the geisha culture.

Day 5: Hakone

- Visit Hakone, a picturesque village renowned for its views of Mount Fuji and hot springs.
- Enjoy a boat ride on Lake Ashi while taking in the gorgeous surroundings.
- For a soothing experience, take a traditional onsen (hot spring) bath in the Owakudani volcanic valley.
- If the weather permits, take in the sights of Mount Fuji.

Day 6: Tokyo

- Spend another day exploring Tokyo or going to any sights you may have missed the first time around.
- Think of going to well-known locations like Meiji Shrine or discovering the energetic districts of Odaiba or Akihabara.
- Indulge in Tokyo's popular culture by perusing electrical stores or going to distinctively designed cafes.

Day 7: Departure

- Depending on your departure time, you can explore Tokyo in the morning or take the opportunity to do some last-minute shopping.
- Depart from Tokyo's international airport to conclude your one-week trip to Japan.

Here is a suggested **weekend itinerary**.

Day 1: Tokyo

- Japan's energetic capital city, Tokyo, is a great place to start your weekend.

- See well-known sites including Asakusa's Sensoji Temple, which is renowned for its exquisite architecture and lively market streets.
- Discover the hip areas of Shibuya and Harajuku, which are well-known for their distinctive cultures, fashions, and shopping.
- Discover the famous Shibuya Crossing, one of the busiest crossings worldwide.
- Savor the evening in neighborhoods with a wide selection of clubs, eateries, and entertainment venues, such as Shinjuku or Roppongi.

Day 2: Day Trip or Further Exploration of Tokyo

- Think about traveling from Tokyo for the day to neighboring cities like Nikko or Kamakura. While Kamakura is home to the well-known Great Buddha statue and exquisite temples, Nikko is renowned for its breathtaking shrines and unspoiled landscape.
- On the other hand, if you'd rather see more of Tokyo, you may stop by places like the Tokyo Skytree, the Meiji Shrine, or the hip Odaiba neighborhood.
- Savor delectable Japanese cuisine in neighborhood eateries or street food stands by sampling specialties like tempura, ramen, and sushi.
- Take in the lively culture of Tokyo and enjoy shopping in popular locations like Ginza or Akihabara, which are known for their electronics and anime, for unique things or mementos (known for high-end shopping).

Chapter 4:
Best Restaurants and Cuisine

Over ages, the culinary culture of Japan has developed into a rich and varied cuisine. A great culinary experience may be had with Japanese cuisine, which emphasizes seasonal ingredients and flavor harmony. The following is an explanation of Japanese food:

The foundation of washoku, or Japanese cuisine, is the idea of serving rice with a variety of okazu, or side dishes. A common sight at Japanese dinners is rice, especially gohan, or steamed white rice, which is sometimes served with pickled vegetables and miso soup. The use of seasonal ingredients guarantees that food is flavorful and fresh. [1].

Japanese cuisine is heavily influenced by seafood because of its coastal setting. Fish is frequently used, whether it be grilled or eaten raw in sushi or sashimi. Popular seafood recipes include oden, which is a simmered dish with fish items in broth, and tempura, which is lightly battered and deep-fried seafood and vegetables. Soba and udon are two popular types of noodles that can be eaten in a variety of ways.

Chinese and Western culinary traditions, among others, have affected Japanese food. Ramen, gyoza, spaghetti, curry, and hamburgers are examples of foreign foods that have been modified to suit Japanese ingredients and tastes. Certain regional cuisines, such as Okinawan taco rice, highlight the blending of Mexican and American culinary elements.

Steamed rice, miso soup, and an assortment of side dishes like pickles, grilled fish, and tamagoyaki (rolled omelets) are typical breakfast fare in traditional Japan. Rice bowls and noodle meals like ramen, soba, and udon can be served for lunch. Usually the largest meal of the day, dinner has a variety of alternatives, including sushi and tori katsu (chicken cutlet). Fresh seafood is frequently used in Japanese cooking; sushi and sashimi are two popular options.

Many classic Japanese meals start with dashi, a soup stock produced from ingredients like kombu (kelp) and katsuobushi (dried bonito flakes). It enhances umami, the fifth fundamental taste that is crucial to Japanese cooking, and flavor depth. Miso, soy sauce, and mirin are further important flavors.

Regional variations are reflected in Japanese food, as each region has its own delicacies. While the Kansai region, which contains towns like Osaka and Kyoto, offers mildly seasoned food, the Kanto region, which includes Tokyo, is renowned for its strong-flavored foods. Local products and cooking methods add to each region's distinct flavors.

With a bowl of rice on the left and a bowl of miso soup on the right, the traditional Japanese table setup places chopsticks between diners. These bowls are positioned behind other dishes. In addition to using chopsticks, Japanese people occasionally use forks, knives, or spoons, depending on the meal being eaten.

Japan boasts the highest number of three-starred Michelin restaurants worldwide, a testament to the popularity and praise of Japanese food around the globe. Japanese culinary masterpieces are widely renowned for their artistry, precision, and attention to detail. In recognition of its cultural importance, Japanese food was added to the UNESCO Intangible Cultural Heritage List in 2013.

In summary, Japanese food emphasizes the flavors of seasonal foods in a wide range of dishes. Japanese cuisine, which includes everything from delicate tempura and powerful noodle bowls to sushi and sashimi, is a delightful exploration of flavor, texture, and harmony. Owing to its broad popularity and cultural significance, this culinary experience is a must-try.

When visiting Japan, there are numerous local dishes that tourists should try to fully experience the country's culinary delights. Here are ten must-try local dishes in Japan and some recommended places to find them:

1. Ginger Pork, or Buta-No-Shogayaki, is a well-known Japanese meal that consists of thinly sliced grilled pork covered with a tasty sauce made with mirin, soy sauce, sake, sliced onions, and ginger. This dish is available at a lot of restaurants, fast food chains, izakayas (traditional Japanese eateries/bars), and even grocery and convenience stores sell bento boxes.
2. Champon is a distinct noodle dish that comes from Nagasaki and differs from ramen. Along with a variety of other ingredients like meat, fish, and veggies, the noodles are cooked right in the soup. It's a must-try dish in Nagasaki and other parts of Japan because of its rich flavors and regional variances.
3. Edamame: Edamame are young soybeans served in their pods; however, they are not a meal in themselves. Usually,

they are grilled or cooked with a small amount of salt added. A favorite appetizer, edamame is served in a lot of izakayas and Japanese eateries across the nation.
4. Fugu: This is a meal that's a must-try for everyone looking for an exciting culinary adventure. Although pufferfish, or fugu, has a reputation for being toxic, when prepared properly, it can be quite tasty. Typically, it's served with specific hot pots or as sashimi. It is advised to try fugu at respectable restaurants where trained chefs meticulously eliminate the harmful components, guaranteeing a tasty and safe dinner.
5. Okonomiyaki is a savory pancake that originates in Osaka. It is constructed with a batter consisting of flour, eggs, grated yam, cabbage, and different toppings such pork, seafood, and vegetables. It's grilled on a griddle and frequently served with seaweed, mayonnaise, bonito flakes, and okonomiyaki sauce on top. All around Japan, okonomiyaki specialized eateries serve this well-liked street cuisine; Osaka is a terrific place to sample the real deal.
6. Another well-known street dish from Osaka is takoyaki, which are spherical, crispy balls stuffed with batter, chopped octopus, and a variety of toppings. They are served hot out of takoyaki pans that are specially made for them. Takoyaki stands and specialty stores can be found in Tokyo, Osaka, and other Japanese cities.
7. Okonomiyaki in the Hiroshima style: Unlike the okonomiyaki found in Osaka, Hiroshima has its own distinct style. Instead of combining the ingredients with the batter, Hiroshima-style okonomiyaki layers the cabbage, noodles, pork, and egg on the griddle. The end product is a dish that highlights the flavors of Hiroshima and is layered and filling. The greatest spot to sample this local delicacy is in Hiroshima.

8. Sushi: One of Japan's most well-known culinary exports, sushi is a must-try during a trip there. Bites-sized bits of rice that has been vinegared and topped with fresh fish or other toppings make up sushi. Sushi is served in many different types of places across the nation, from upscale sushiya (sushi restaurants) to conveyor belt sushi restaurants (kaiten-zushi).
9. Ramen: Ramen is a thick noodle soup meal with many regional variations that is famously good in Japan. Every area has a distinct way of preparing ramen, including differences in the flavors, toppings, broth, and noodles. Every food enthusiast should experience the local ramen, whether it's the rich miso ramen from Hokkaido, the Tokyo-style shoyu ramen, or the tonkotsu ramen from Kyushu. In Japan, there are many distinct types of ramen eateries, ranging from local operations to well-known chains.
10. Kobe Conflict: For those who enjoy meat, Kobe beef is a must-try delicacy because of its outstanding quality and global reputation. Raised in Hyogo Prefecture, Tajima cattle are the source of Kobe beef, which is highly valued for its rich flavor, marbling, and tenderness. Sukiyaki, teppanyaki, and steak are among the Kobe beef dishes that are served at a lot of upscale restaurants in Kobe and neighboring places.

When visiting Japan, there are plenty of affordable eatery options for visitors apart from traditional restaurants. Here are various options to consider:

- Donburi restaurants: Rice bowl meals from Donburi chains like Yoshinoya, Sukiya, and Matsuya are reasonably priced and delicious. They provide set meals (tei-shoku) and specialties like gyudon (beef rice bowl) at reasonably priced pricing.

- Yatai (Street Stalls): Yatai are improvised street stalls where you can get tasty meals at reasonable prices. They serve a wide range of foods, including ramen, yakiniku, oden, and yakisoba. Yatai offers a homey and genuine dining experience, frequently with compact seating spaces.
- Markets and stores during time-dependent sales: In Japan, markets and stores frequently host time-dependent sales during which you can discover reduced food goods. Bento shops and supermarkets usually offer discounted prices on bentos (lunch boxes) in the evenings before they close. This enables you to have a satisfying supper for a much lower cost.
- Convenience stores: Known as konbini in the local dialect, these establishments are common in Japan and provide a large selection of reasonably priced food alternatives. In addition to ready-to-eat meals, they also sell snacks, sandwiches, and onigiri (rice balls). Convenience store chains that are well-known include Lawson, Family Mart, and 7-Eleven. These stores provide affordable and speedy options for meals or snacks.
- Ramen bars: In Japan, ramen is a well-liked and reasonably priced cuisine. A wide range of flavors and styles are available at affordable costs at ramen bars. Ordinary ramen bowls range in price from 300 to 500 yen. Even Michelin-starred ramen is available at some places for only 1,000 yen.
- Coco Ichibanya: Located all throughout Japan, Coco Ichibanya is an inexpensive curry restaurant. They provide delectable, spicily-varying Japanese curry. It's a fantastic choice for tasty meals that are reasonably priced.
- Restaurants serving Okonomiyaki: Okonomiyaki is a popular savory pancake in Japan. Affordable and delicious okonomiyaki is served in eateries all around the nation, but particularly in Osaka and Hiroshima. You can add extra

toppings and ingredients to your okonomiyaki at these places to make it uniquely yours.
- Restaurants for families (Famiresu): Both locals and visitors enjoy eating at family-friendly establishments including Café Gusto, Denny's, and Jonathan's. They provide a large selection of reasonably priced Western and Asian-style cuisine. For a few hundred yen, family eateries offer limitless soft drinks and coffee, making them an affordable eating choice.
- Happy hours at izakayas: During certain hours of the day, a lot of izakayas, or traditional Japanese pubs, provide happy hour deals. You can take advantage of cheap food products and drinks. Izakayas are renowned for their vibrant ambiance and wide selection of shareable small plates (izakaya-style foods) on their menu.
- Department shops in Japan frequently offer basement dining halls or food courts where you can get a great variety of reasonably priced and mouthwatering meals. There are many different cuisines available at these food courts, such as Japanese, Chinese, Korean, and Western, giving you a variety of selections at affordable prices.

By exploring these affordable eatery options in Japan, visitors can enjoy delicious meals without straining their budget. Whether it's street stalls, convenience stores, or specialized eateries, there are plenty of choices to suit different tastes and preferences.

Here are ten renowned restaurants in Japan and their renowned dishes:

1. Tokyo's Ninja Akasaka is a restaurant with a ninja motif that provides a distinctive dining experience. The menu offers items that resemble star blades as well as a culinary recreation of a tiny Zen garden. At your table, the

performers do ninja maneuvers. Japanese cuisine is wonderful and paired with an engaging dining experience.
2. Tokyo's Shunsai Tempura Arima is a specialty restaurant serving tempura, a well-known Japanese meal comprising battered and deep-fried fish or vegetables. They provide a selection of tempura prepared with fresh ingredients such prawns, yams, white fish, and asparagus. The tempura is flavorful, crunchy, and light.
3. Tokyo's Kobe Beef Kaiseki 511 is a restaurant that specializes in serving the well-known Kobe beef. The Tajima type of Japanese black cow produces Kobe meat, which is prized for its tenderness and marbling. To guarantee the best quality meat, the chef personally chooses the cows at this restaurant. The Kobe beef is expertly prepared and presented in delectable dishes.
4. Den (Tokyo): Known for its outstanding flavors and ingredients, Den is a Michelin-starred restaurant in Tokyo. Zaiyu Hasegawa, the proprietor, specializes in inventive Japanese home cooking. A selection of items on the menu highlight the chef's creativity and attention to detail.
5. Tokyo's Sukiyabashi Jiro is a well-known sushi restaurant with a global reputation. It is renowned for its meticulous attention to detail and traditional sushi artistry. Three Michelin stars have been bestowed upon Jiro Ono, the owner and sushi expert. With omakase-style meals that highlight the best and freshest ingredients, the restaurant provides a distinctive sushi experience.
6. Tokyo's Ryugin is a three-Michelin-starred restaurant renowned for its creative and inventive take on Japanese food. Chef Seiji Yamamoto creates dishes that are visually striking and unusual by fusing traditional Japanese flavors with modern techniques. The restaurant serves multi-course meals that highlight the greatest produce available at that time of year.

7. Kikunoi (Kyoto) is a renowned kaiseki restaurant located in Kyoto. A typical multi-course meal called kaiseki is served that changes with the seasons. Kikunoi provides exceptional kaiseki dining experiences, where meals are carefully prepared with the best seasonal ingredients. Three Michelin stars have been bestowed upon the restaurant.
8. Tokyo's well-known kaiseki restaurant is called Ishikawa. Chef Hideki Ishikawa is renowned for his commitment to maintaining age-old Japanese cooking methods. With exquisitely presented dishes that accentuate the natural flavors of the ingredients, the restaurant provides a sophisticated dining experience. Three Michelin stars have been bestowed upon Ishikawa.
9. Sushi Saito (Tokyo): One of Tokyo's most famous sushi restaurants is Sushi Saito. Takashi Saito, a sushi expert known for his skill and dedication to excellence, is in charge of it. With just a few chairs, the restaurant provides a cozy eating experience. The best and freshest seafood is included on the omakase-style menu.
10. Kyubey (Tokyo): With a lengthy history, Kyubey is a well-known sushi restaurant in Tokyo. It is well-known for serving classic Edo-style sushi, which places a strong emphasis on using seasonal and fresh ingredients. Kyubey's talented sushi chefs craft exquisite sushi that accentuates the inherent tastes of fish and seafood.

These renowned restaurants offer a range of exquisite dishes that represent the best of Japanese cuisine. Each restaurant provides a unique dining experience and showcases the culinary expertise of their respective chefs.

Chapter 5: Accommodations in Japan

When looking for affordable accommodation options in Japan apart from hotels, there are several choices available. Here are some options to consider:

- Hostels: For tourists on a tight budget, particularly those seeking a lively and sociable environment, hostels are an affordable choice. Hostels provide shared rooms in the style of dorms with communal spaces like restrooms. They are an excellent method to meet other tourists and get lodging at a lower cost.
- Guest Homes: Known by another name, minshuku, guest houses are traditional Japanese housing options that offer reasonably priced lodging with a regional flavor. These are family-run businesses with basic accommodation and communal amenities. You can fully immerse yourself in the local culture and enjoy the gracious hospitality of Japanese families by booking a guest house.
- Traditional Japanese inns known as "ryokans" provide a distinctive cultural experience. There are ryokans that are

affordable, even if some of them can be pricey. These low-cost ryokans still include the customary futon beds, communal bathrooms, and tatami mat floors, but they could have smaller rooms or fewer amenities.
- In Japan, capsule hotels offer a unique lodging choice, particularly for individuals traveling alone. These lodging establishments offer compact, private sleeping pods furnished with a bed, TV, and occasionally minimal conveniences. Although they are small, capsule hotels provide a handy and reasonably priced spot to rest and refuel.
- Business Hotels: Business hotels provide reasonably priced lodging options and are tailored to meet the demands of business visitors. They feature small rooms with basic facilities including a bed, desk, and private bathroom and are typically found close to rail stations. For tourists on a tight budget, business hotels make sense.
- Camping: You can set up a tent and take in the scenery at any of the many parks and outdoor spaces found throughout Japan. Camping is an affordable choice, particularly for those who enjoy the great outdoors. A few campgrounds offer cooking facilities, restrooms, and recreational opportunities.
- Airbnb and guesthouses: Using websites such as Airbnb to rent out flats or private rooms might be less expensive than staying in a hotel. Depending on your tastes and budget, a variety of options are available, ranging from shared rooms to complete apartments. Furthermore, guesthouses that are advertised on websites like Airbnb provide a combination of conventional and contemporary lodging.
- Volunteer Programs: In exchange for volunteering, a number of Japanese organizations offer volunteer labor that includes free or heavily subsidized lodging. This keeps lodging expenses down while still enabling visitors to

- become fully immersed in local communities and make significant contributions to worthwhile organizations.
- Always remember to reserve lodging well in advance, particularly in renowned tourist destinations like Tokyo and Kyoto and during the busiest travel seasons. Examine and contrast costs, go through other travelers' opinions, and think about the location and facilities that fit your demands and price range.
- It's crucial to remember that these accommodations may not always be available and may cost different amounts. It is advised to search multiple booking websites, such Booking.com, Hostelworld, or Airbnb, to identify the most reasonably priced choices that satisfy your needs.
- These five hotels in Japan are well-known for their facilities and reasonable prices:
- The compact rooms of the APA Hotel Tokyo Shiomi Ekimae (Tokyo) are furnished with modern amenities including free Wi-Fi, flat-screen TVs, and private bathrooms. It provides easy access to the city's main attractions and is conveniently located near to Shiomi Station.
- Near Kyoto Station, the Daiwa Roynet Hotel Kyoto-Hachijoguchi (Kyoto) has comfortable accommodations with complimentary WiFi, air conditioning, and flat-screen TVs. It also has a restaurant and convenient access to some of Kyoto's most well-known landmarks.
- The hotel Dormy Inn Premium Shibuya Jingumae (Tokyo) is well-known for its hot spring baths, which provide guests a peaceful environment. The rooms are completely equipped with flat-screen TVs, comfortable beds, and free Wi-Fi. It's close to retail and entertainment venues in the trendy Shibuya district.
- The large, modern rooms at Hotel Mystays Premier Omori (Tokyo) are intended to make visitors feel at home. The rooms come equipped with kitchenettes, complimentary

Wi-Fi, and flat-screen TVs. It is well located near to Omori Station and offers easy access to all of Tokyo's attractions.
- The bustling Shinjuku neighborhood is home to the Hotel MyStays Nishi Shinjuku (Tokyo), which offers budget accommodations with kitchenettes, flat-screen TVs, and free WiFi. It is near Shinjuku Station and provides easy access to dining, shopping, and entertainment options.
- The Mitsui Garden Hotel Hiroshima in Hiroshima provides comfortable lodgings equipped with complimentary Wi-Fi, air conditioning, and flat-screen TVs. There's a restaurant, bar, and front desk open around-the-clock. The hotel's convenient location near Hiroshima Station makes it an excellent place to start exploring the city.
- In the renowned Asakusa district of Tokyo, the Richmond Hotel Premier Asakusa International offers modern, stylish accommodations complete with air conditioning, flat-screen TVs, and free WiFi. It has a front desk that is available 24/7, a restaurant, and a bar. Walking distance from the hotel is the Senso-ji Temple and other popular attractions.
- Near Kyoto Station, the comfortable accommodations of the Rihga Royal Hotel Kyoto (Kyoto) provide air conditioning, flat-screen TVs, and complimentary WiFi. It offers a swimming pool, fitness center, and assortment of restaurants. When it comes to seeing Kyoto's cultural attractions, the hotel is a great place to start.
- Sotetsu Fresa Inn Tokyo-Kinshicho (Tokyo) - This hotel offers well-appointed, compact rooms with free Wi-Fi, flat-screen TVs, and private bathrooms. It offers easy access to Tokyo Disneyland and other city attractions and is adjacent to Kinshicho Station.
- Osaka Umeda Higashi Toyoko Inn (Osaka) To ensure guests enjoy a comfortable stay, this hotel offers reasonably priced rooms with free Wi-Fi, flat-screen TVs, and air

conditioning. It offers quick access to Osaka's leisure and business areas and is situated close to Umeda Station.

Chapter 6:
Cultural Activities in Japan

Japan is a nation steeped in heritage and culture, providing travelers with a wide variety of cultural experiences to enjoy while traveling there.

Here are 15 cultural activities that tourists in Japan must try to enjoy:

Take a Walk Around Historic Townscapes Donning a Kimono: Take in the allure of bygone eras in Japan by donning a kimono and touring sites of historical significance in places like Kyoto and Asakusa in Tokyo.

Visit one of Japan's more than 3,000 hot springs, or "onsen," to unwind, take advantage of the many health advantages, and take in a traditional aspect of Japanese culture. Hakone, Kinosaki, and Shizuoka are a few well-known onsen destinations.

Enjoy a Traditional Matsuri to Celebrate the Japanese Way: Traditional festivals, or matsuri, are held all throughout Japan and feature street cuisine, music, dances, parades, and traditional dances. Take in the vibrant ambiance and fully submerge yourself in traditional Japanese culture.

Stay in a Traditional Ryokan to Experience Japanese Hospitality: Tatami rooms, futons, and natural hot springs are all features of ryokans, a type of traditional inn. A wonderful stay and an insight into Japanese culture are offered by ryokans.

Discover the Fundamentals of a Japanese Tea Ceremony: Take part in a traditional Japanese tea ceremony, which is a methodical and ceremonial procedure that exemplifies Japan's attention to detail and detail-oriented culture. In large cities, take a beginner's course to learn the basics of preparing and appreciating tea.

Experience Life Like a Monk at a Shukubo Temple: Spend time at a shukubo, a temple hostel, to gain insight into Buddhism. Eat Buddhist food, take part in daily activities, and discover the spiritual practices. Wakayama Prefecture's Koyasan is a well-known location for this experience.

See Geisha Performances: Take in the sights and sounds of authentic Japanese entertainment by attending geisha performances. These talented craftspeople reside and train in geisha homes in certain places, like Kyoto. Meeting them can be arranged through a number of organizations.

Discover the National Sport of Japan: See a sumo match, a popular traditional sport in Japan with a history spanning over 1,500 years. Watch as sumo wrestlers battle to push one another out of the ring, showcasing their strength and ability (dohyo).

Participate in Local Celebrations (Matsuri): Take part in matsuri, which are Japanese festivities that feature food booths, traditional attire, dances, and processions in addition to local customs. The Gion Matsuri in Kyoto, the Summer Matsuri with pyrotechnics, and the Snow Festival in Sapporo are a few prominent festivities.

Learn the Japanese flower-arranging technique known as ikebana, which is renowned for its simplicity and minimalism. To have a rudimentary understanding of this old art form, take a beginner's lesson in one of the major towns.

Take in the Big Beat of Taiko Drumming: See the potent rhythms that have resonated throughout Japanese history by attending a taiko drumming concert. Several locations provide hands-on sessions where guests can practice playing the taiko drums.

Explore Calligraphy: Learn how to write kanji characters with conventional brushes and ink by taking a stab at Japanese calligraphy, or "shodo." Enroll in a calligraphy course to delve into the creative and contemplative facets of this age-old art form.

Discover Samurai Culture: To gain insight into the fascinating world of the samurai, visit venues associated to the samurai, such as museums and old castles. There are locations that provide "samurai experiences," where you can put on samurai armor and practice using a sword.

Take in a kabuki performance to learn more about the world of this historic Japanese theatrical genre, which is renowned for its ornate costumes, stylized acting, and narrative. Discover the distinct fusion of dance, music, and theater that makes kabuki such an enthralling cultural event.

See Traditional Crafts Villages: Discover traditional Japanese craftsmanship by visiting villages such as Takayama, Shirakawago, and Kanazawa. Here, you may watch artisans at work. These towns provide interactive workshops where you may learn how to make ceramics, lacquerware, and silk fabrics.

Through immersive encounters and a glimpse into Japan's rich legacy, these cultural activities enable visitors to understand and participate in traditional Japanese culture.

Chapter 7:
Nightlife And Festivals In Japan

- Japan offers a vibrant and diverse nightlife scene in many places. Travelers may enjoy a range of nighttime events and activities, from bustling metropolises to traditional entertainment hotspots. Here are a few of the top tourist destinations in Japan for nightlife:
- Tokyo: The city has a thriving nightlife with lots of alternatives, such as hip clubs in Roppongi and Shibuya, small-town pubs in Golden Gai, and live music venues in Shimokitazawa.
- Osaka: Known for its bustling Dotonbori entertainment district, Osaka is well-known for its exciting nightlife. Along the canal are street food vendors, clubs, pubs, and karaoke for visitors to enjoy.
- Kyoto: Although its ancient treasures are its main draw, Kyoto has a distinctive nightlife. Kyoto's Gion neighborhood is well-known for its traditional tea houses, where guests may take in geisha performances and experience the local way of life.

- Nagoya: Sakae and Osu are two of the city's popular entertainment districts, and the city boasts a vibrant nightlife scene. In the lively dining scene of the city, visitors may also savor local specialties and izakaya in the style of Nagoya.
- Hiroshima: Hiroshima has a carefree and easygoing nightlife. Along Nagarekawa's picturesque riverfront are waterfront restaurants, jazz clubs, and traditional Japanese pubs, or izakayas.
- Sapporo: The Susukino neighborhood, which is well-known for its abundance of pubs, clubs, and eateries, is the hub of the city's nightlife. Famous beer from Sapporo, a lively nightlife, and winter festivals like the Snow Festival in February are all available to visitors.
- Fukuoka: With exciting neighborhoods like Tenjin and Nakasu, Fukuoka has a bustling nightlife. There are many different nightlife alternatives available to visitors, such as bars, clubs, yatai (food vendors), and local specialties.
- Yokohama: The Minato Mirai neighborhood is the hub of the city's nightlife, featuring a wide range of entertainment options including pubs, clubs, and eateries with breathtaking waterfront views. In the evening, visitors can also take in Chinatown's lively environment.
- Kobe: A lot of jazz clubs and bars in Kobe offer live jazz performances, and the city is well-known for its lively jazz scene. In addition, visitors can take advantage of a wide range of culinary alternatives and explore Sannomiya's vibrant entertainment zone.
- Nagasaki: With its historical appeal, Nagasaki provides a distinct nightlife experience. In addition to exploring izakayas and taking in the city's nighttime vistas from Mount Inasa, visitors can relish the lively ambiance of the Hamanomachi district.

- Sendai: The heart of the city's nightlife is the Kokuboncho neighborhood, which is well-known for its vibrant pubs, clubs, and performance spaces. Tourists can take advantage of the city's exciting nightlife and discover the regional cuisine.
- Naha (Okinawa): Naha provides a distinctive fusion of contemporary and traditional nightlife. Wander along the bustling Kokusai Street, which is lined with eateries, bars, and gift shops, or visit nearby venues to see traditional Okinawan music and dance performances.
- Hakodate: With a wide range of pubs, eateries, and izakayas, Hakodate's nightlife is concentrated around the Bay Area. Explore the city's historic Motomachi neighborhood, take in the breathtaking nighttime views from Mount Hakodate, and savor the excellent seafood the city has to offer.
- Kanazawa: Known for its traditional tea houses and geisha culture, the Higashi Chaya neighborhood is the hub of Kanazawa's nightlife. In addition to visiting local eateries and bars, tourists can take part in a traditional tea ceremony and discover the local sake scene.
- Matsumoto: Matsumoto provides a more relaxed atmosphere for nightlife. Travelers can visit neighborhood izakayas to taste local specialties, explore the city's quaint bars and pubs, and take in live musical performances.

Now, here are 15 main festivals in Japan and some activities that visitors enjoy:

1. Sapporo Snow Festival (February, Sapporo): Enjoy winter sports, feast on delectable food, and marvel at the breathtaking snow and ice creations.
2. Gion Matsuri (July): This well-known celebration takes place in Kyoto and includes street cuisine, music, dance,

and processions of traditional floats. It is possible for tourists to fully engage in traditional Kyoto culture.
3. Nebuta Matsuri: Held in August in Aomori, this festival features enormous, colorful illuminated floats known as "nebuta," accompanied by traditional dance performances and music. Guests are welcome to take part in the exciting celebrations and see the magnificent parade.
4. One of Tokyo's biggest festivals, Kanda Matsuri takes place in May and includes dance performances, traditional music, and processions of elaborate portable shrines. Guests are welcome to explore the ancient Kanda district and take in the vibrant atmosphere.
5. Takayama Event (April and October): This festival, which is well-known for its intricate floats, gives guests the chance to take in traditional dances and music as well as local cuisine and sake.
6. Tokushima hosts the well-known dance event Awa Odori in August, during which participants dance traditional dances in the streets. In addition to taking in the vibrant performances and local cuisine, visitors can dance.
7. Large phallic statues are paraded during the distinctive Kanamara Matsuri celebration, held in April in Kawasaki. The festival honors fertility. In addition to taking part in the celebrations, visitors may savor regional cuisine and take in the vibrant environment.
8. Tanabata Matsuri, sometimes called the Star Festival, is celebrated in August in Sendai and honors the union of two celestial lovers. In addition to trying local street cuisine, visitors may take in traditional musical performances and vibrant décor.
9. Kishiwada Danjiri Matsuri (September), an exuberant celebration in Osaka, is characterized by the pulling of big wooden carts through the streets amid upbeat

performances and shouts. Guests are welcome to take part in the celebrations and observe the excitement.

10. Chichibu Yomatsuri (December): This celebration in Saitama features amazing floats that are lit up with thousands of lanterns, creating a mystical ambiance. The holiday atmosphere, customary entertainment, and fireworks are available to visitors.
11. Kōchi Yosakoi Matsuri (August): This contemporary festival creates a lively and lively ambiance by fusing traditional dance with new music. Viewers may take in the exciting acts and experience the festival vibe.
12. August in Tokyo is Asakusa Samba Carnival, a bright carnival with samba dancers, upbeat music, and colorful costumes. Guests are welcome to participate in the exciting street celebration and take in the exciting acts.
13. Hirosaki Cherry Blossom Festival (April, Hirosaki): In addition to taking part at traditional tea ceremonies, musical performances, and parades, visitors can enjoy the breathtaking cherry blossoms in Hirosaki Park.
14. Yuki Matsuri (February): A winter celebration in Yokote that includes candlelit snow tunnels and kamakura (snow cottages). Visitors can sample local cuisine, visit the snow sculptures, and go on snow slides.
15. May sees the historical event of Aoi Matsuri in Kyoto, where attendees parade in full regalia reminiscent of the Heian era. Viewers can take in the refined ambiance and listen to traditional music.

Chapter 8:
Souvenirs And Shopping in Japan

Shopping in Japan is a delightful experience, offering a wide range of options for visitors. Here are some places to shop in Japan, along with tips for visitors and must-buy souvenirs:

1. 100 yen shop (Daiso): Daiso is a well-known 100 yen shop that offers a range of reasonably priced items, such as food, household supplies, and adorable trinkets. It's a terrific location to shop on a budget and has several branches throughout Japan.
2. Don Quijote: Also called "Donki," this multi-story retailer has a variety of goods, such as food, apparel, electronics, and one-of-a-kind trinkets. You can find a lot of interesting and unusual things there.
3. Asakusa (Nakamise Shopping Street): Asakusa is a famous shopping district in Tokyo that is well-known for its assortment of Japanese mementos, including green tea, chopsticks, hand fans, and ornaments. It's the ideal location to purchase traditional Japanese products.
4. Another name for Kappabashi is "Chefs' Paradise." Tokyo's Kappabashi Street is known for its kitchen and tableware

stores. Chefs frequently shop there since it has a large selection of cooking supplies, including Japanese knives.
5. Tokyo's Harajuku is well-known for its distinctive street style and high fashion. It's an excellent location for clothing shopping, particularly for youth. In addition, freshly fried potato chips and limited-edition Japanese delicacies are available at Calbee Plus in Harajuku.
6. Akihabara: Akihabara is the center of otaku culture and electronics. It's the ideal location to purchase electrical devices, video games, manga, and products associated with anime. A large selection of affordable electronic devices is available.
7. Narita Airport: Narita International Airport is a convenient location for last-minute shopping if you're pressed for time. It boasts a large number of gift stores with a wide range of merchandise, such as food, candies, apparel, makeup, and electronics.

Tips for Shopping in Japan:

- If you want to shop tax-free, bring your passport. Visitors can shop tax-free at many stores, and by displaying your passport, you can get a 10% discount on your purchases.
- Verify the store's opening times. Certain stores could have varying hours of operation or close on particular days.
- Pay attention to customs laws. Make sure you understand your home country's customs laws so that the things you buy can be lawfully returned.
- Think about the room for your bags. To be sure the things you buy will fit in your luggage, consider their weight and size.

Must-Buy Souvenirs in Japan:

- Matcha Green Tea: Specialty tea shops and department stores sell premium matcha green tea.
- Traditional Kimono: To find stunning kimonos, visit stores that sell traditional apparel or department stores.
- Japanese Snacks: For a broad selection of Japanese snacks, visit department stores or specialty snack shops.
- Sake: Look for department stores or sake-specific specialized shops that provide a large assortment of sake.
- Japanese Ceramics: To find distinctive Japanese ceramics, visit pottery shops or specialist stores.
- Origami Paper: For a large selection of origami paper, visit craft stores or stationery stores.
- Japanese Kitchen Knives: To find premium Japanese knives, check out specialty knife shops or kitchenware stores.
- Maneki-neko (Lucky Cat): Look for many varieties of Maneki-neko at department stores or specialized souvenir shops.
- Japanese Beauty Products: To find well-liked Japanese beauty products, head to department stores or cosmetic stores.
- Wagashi (Japanese sweets): For exquisitely made Japanese sweets, visit department stores or traditional sweet shops.
- Traditional Crafts: Seek out specialty shops or craft stores that sell lacquerware and woodworking, two examples of traditional Japanese crafts.
- Hakama, or traditional Japanese clothing: To find traditional hakama, visit department stores or specialist shops.
- Furoshiki (Traditional Wrapping Cloth): For a wide selection of furoshiki, visit department stores or specialist shops.

- Tenugui (Japanese hand towels): Department stores and gift shops have a large selection of tenugui.
- Items Made of Yuzen or Chusen Fabric: To find items made of Yuzen or Chusen fabric, visit department stores or specialty fabric stores.

Chapter 9:
Tips For Traveling in Japan

Here are 15 tips for tourists in Japan to save money, time, and make the most of their visit:

1. Invest in a Japan Rail Pass (JR Pass) to avoid paying excessive transportation expenditures. The JR Pass offers unlimited travel on JR trains, including the bullet train.
2. Utilize the JR Rail Lines in urban areas: You can save money on local transportation by using the JR Pass on the JR train lines that are available in many Japanese cities.
3. Walk or bike: To save money on transportation and to take in the local flavor, choose to walk or cycle when exploring cities.
4. Take the bus: Although they could take longer, buses can be a more cost-effective option than bullet trains for local travel in Japan.

5. Make a thoughtful itinerary: To cut down on travel time and costs, visit sites together in the same vicinity.
6. Make use of free or heavily discounted tourist passes: A lot of cities provide discounted passes for attractions and public transit. Look around and evaluate choices to locate the top offers.
7. Stay in a cheap hotel: If you want to save money on lodging, think about booking a room at a hostel, guesthouse, or cheap hotel. Airbnb is a good alternative as well.
8. Eat at neighborhood eateries and izakayas: For more reasonably priced and genuine Japanese food, seek for tiny, neighborhood restaurants rather than tourist hotspots. Japanese-style taverns called izakayas frequently serve economically priced food and beverages.
9. Try food stands and convenience stores: FamilyMart, Lawson, and other similar establishments provide a range of reasonably priced ready-to-eat meals, snacks, and beverages. Yatai, or food stalls, are located in certain locations and offer mouthwatering street cuisine at more affordable costs.
10. Take advantage of lunch specials: A lot of eateries provide reasonably priced lunch sets or specials that let you sample a variety of Japanese dishes for less money.
11. Investigate regional markets: For affordable fresh vegetables, snacks, and souvenirs, visit local markets like Tokyo's Tsukiji Fish Market or Kyoto's Nishiki Market.
12. See free sites: Parks, shrines, temples, and gardens are just a few of the many free sites in Japan. Use these to your advantage to cut costs while getting a taste of Japanese culture.
13. Participate in free cultural events: Seek out complimentary cultural events, including tea ceremonies, calligraphy lessons, or customary shows, provided by cultural institutions or travel agencies.

14. Get your tickets at a discount in advance: To save money and beat long lines, think about purchasing discounted tickets online or in advance for popular attractions like museums or amusement parks.
15. Shop at 100-yen stores and neighborhood markets: Daiso and other 100-yen stores provide reasonably priced mementos, everyday essentials, and snacks. Look for unusual and reasonably priced presents at your local markets.

By implementing these tips, tourists in Japan can save money, optimize their time, and have a memorable and budget-friendly experience in the country.

Conclusion

Japan is a fascinating tourist destination that offers an abundance of historical sites, a lively culture, stunning landscapes, and delicious food. Whether a visitor wants to explore the ancient temples of Kyoto, stroll through the bustling streets of Tokyo, or take in the spectacular natural beauty of Hokkaido, Japan has something to offer everyone. Even though traveling to Japan used to seem expensive, there are ways to cut costs, such as by using the Japan Rail Pass, finding a cheap lodging, and dining at neighborhood restaurants. Japan is a popular travel destination since it is also well-known for being safe. Remember to plan your itinerary carefully, take in the free attractions, and fully immerse yourself in the unique experiences that Japan has to offer. Japan is sure to wow anyone who enjoys fine food, culture, the outdoors, or history — it will provide you with unforgettable experiences.

Travelers are generally fascinated by the range of experiences that Japan has to offer, and it is simple to have a memorable trip without going over budget with careful planning and cost-conscious judgments. So get ready for an experience that will never fade as you explore Japan's treasures.

Printed in Great Britain
by Amazon